Confessions of a Swinger

By Karen Kennedy

Printed in Victoria, Canada

National Library of Canada Cataloguing in Publication

Kennedy, Karen, 1961-
      Confessions of a swinger : reflections on bipolar
affective disorder or manic depression / Karen Kennedy.

ISBN 1-4120-0284-2

      1. Kennedy, Karen, 1961- —Health. 2. Manic-depres-
sive persons—Canada—Biography. I. Title.

RC516.K463 2003   616.89'5'0092   C2003-902575-6

TRAFFORD

This book was published *on-demand* in cooperation with Trafford Publishing. On-demand publishing is a unique process and service of making a book available for retail sale to the public taking advantage of on-demand manufacturing and Internet marketing. **On-demand publishing** includes promotions, retail sales, manufacturing, order fulfilment, accounting and collecting royalties on behalf of the author.

Suite 6E, 2333 Government St., Victoria, B.C. V8T 4P4, CANADA

Phone	250-383-6864	Toll-free	1-888-232-4444 (Canada & US)
Fax	250-383-6804	E-mail	sales@trafford.com
Web site	www.trafford.com	TRAFFORD PUBLISHING IS A DIVISION OF TRAFFORD
HOLDINGS LTD.			
Trafford Catalogue #03-0653		www.trafford.com/robots/03-0653.html	

10   9   8   7   6   5   4

Author's Note

This book is not based on research but rather personal experience and potential explanation.

Dear Reader,

It is important to understand the genesis of this book. In fact, it was never intended to be a book per se, but more of a laying out of the pieces of a puzzled life in an attempt to get a glimpse of the larger picture. As I wrote in each chapter how my illness impacted my life and those around me, I would try to relate my experience of particular symptoms of either depressive or manic episodes to commonly known facts and diagnostic criteria found on this subject. In it's rough stages, I would recount events that I believe were influenced by my undiagnosed illness and then catalogue potential symptoms, warning signs or possible medical explanation in a section which would later become "Insights into Manic Depressive Illness" found at the end of most chapters in Confessions of a Swinger. This endeavor was purely a personal attempt. Consequently you will not find a bibliography. I was not compelled to compile sources of my information except to say that these "insights" or information was gleaned from the many conversations I had with my psychiatrist Dr. C. Ryder. I was also insatiable in my quest for information on mental illness and read many books and pamphlets that helped me understand what I was dealing with.

Please, however, know that this material has been read and cleared for accuracy by professionals in the field of mental health.

On that note, this book is also not intended as material in which to make a diagnosis but most importantly to encourage those who feel they may have a mental health issue to seek help from their doctor.

Yours,

Karen Kennedy

We have all been given Divine blessings...
some more challenging
than others and harder to recognize...
but Divine nonetheless.

Acknowledgments

*A profound thank you to those family and friends who chose
to be a part of my journey, especially my daughter
and son whose unconditional love gave it greater meaning.*

*My gratitude also to Rany, Susan, Ron and of course Dr. C. Ryder,
for motivating and enabling me to share my story with you.*

Confessions of a Swinger

"*Confessions of a Swinger*"
Foreword

Our society can go a long way in reducing the stigma associated with mental illness by gaining a better understanding and knowledge on mental health issues. One in five Canadians will experience a mental health issue which will affect their quality of life. Governments, businesses and society as a whole will pay a large price as long as adequate effort is not made to understand and address mental health and mental illness issues. Depression has been acknowledged as one of the most common psychiatric disorders. It is estimated that by the year 2020, depression will be the leading cause of disability affecting the workplace worldwide.

As a human race we openly discuss cancer, heart problems, diabetes, a broken leg or arm, kidney disease and a myriad of other physical illnesses. We show interest, send cards or flowers to someone that has had heart surgery, survived cancer; we call to ask how they are doing. But when it comes to someone that has a disease of the brain, our guard goes up. Is the brain not considered to be part of the human body? Most of the time we are unaware that an acquaintance, a friend or even a family member, are silently dealing with a mental illness. Stigma prevails, ignorance reigns and an environment of not knowing what to do or how to respond, blossoms. Mental illness is a chemical imbalance of the brain; diabetes is a chemical imbalance of the pancreas; we openly talk about having diabetes, or of someone else having diabetes but when it comes to a mood disorder, or schizophrenia or clinical depression – just to mention a few – we clam up most of the time.

It takes courageous individuals like Karen Kennedy to try and make a significant dent into the wall of silence that surrounds mental illness. In

6

her book Karen openly discusses her turbulent journey with a mood disorder. Her experience was like sailing in rough waters in a one man boat without a compass or a port-of-call. All through her book, Karen exhibits an excellent sense of humour, writing about a subject that is not even remotely funny. Having a mental illness may contribute to loss of employment, loss of relationships, loss of pleasure, loss of all the little things in life that we take for granted; and that is not funny.

Finally, "Confessions of a Swinger" is a book about hope, about how one determined woman got to the root of her problem and started dealing with it. It's about recovery and resilience, and about an ongoing struggle with mental illness. A mood disorder did not stop Karen from having a career, a family, friends, a life. To quote Karen "It is immensely easier to live with the devil you know than the devil you don't know". The unknown generates fear for most of us. However, once we know what we are dealing with, we may still feel the fear, but we are able to move on.

Myths and misunderstandings around mental illness have contributed to negative judgments, shame and stigma. Karen through her personal insights helps to dispel some of these myths, to "normalize" mental illness and to have it "emerge into light".

Rany Xanthopoulo
Director of Development,
Education and Administration

Canadian Mental Health Association
Lambton County Branch

CONFESSIONS of a SWINGER

Introduction to My Story

Politically incorrect as some would say, I feel a compelling need to apologize for my life, as it was, in those tumultuous years. I also want to make amends, in advance, for hurt feelings that may come about as a result of this book. The people I suspect will be disturbed by my disclosures, are the members of my immediate and extended family. I thank God these things were revealed five years into my second marriage, because had they previous to, I'm sure my in-laws would have found a way to have me hospitalized until their son was deprogrammed and on his was to some foreign country. Stephen's parents biggest concern at that point, before the wedding, was that I wasn't Jewish. If they only knew! As it stands now, I have shared most of the more extraordinary moments of my life with my mother-in-law. I figure some things are best finding out directly and not through reading in a book. The evening after these revelations were made, I found myself mired in misgivings. I was terrified Stephen's mother would see me differently, defective. Although I never tried to be anyone other than who I am, I couldn't help but feel like an imposter exposed. I called her that night to express these fears and realized they were unfounded. As it was, my disclosure had explained some of my questionable previous behavior. My mother-in-law knew there was something not quite right at times, but was too discrete to inquire.

She assured me that my history was not indicative to her of who I truly was. Indeed, she was surprised that I could have behaved in the ways I described. It was so unlike me, she said. Yes, that was my point, I was ill at those times.

We are very much alike, she and I, especially in the way we both enjoy reading medical books for pleasure, so she was not completely unfamiliar with the condition of manic-depression. But she emphasized that she saw me as a good person, mother and spouse to her son, and the fact that

I had this illness would not change her opinion. These words meant a great deal to me. For one, she is a wonderful, bright and spirited woman whom I greatly admire, and two, there was still a chance I would be in the will!

And then, of course, there is my immediate family. Truthfully, I am not too concerned about the reactions of my sisters, after reading this book. Despite being both geographically and chronologically distanced from them for many years, there is closeness between us. Overall, there was never contention over one of us being better, smarter or luckier than the others. We are who we are. But my mother, well, she's a different story. The early years weren't particularly harmonious, but our relationship has seen profound changes. I have achieved a deep love and acceptance for my mother for all that she is and was in the past. I am proud of the fact that I can verbalize these feelings and am confident she accepts them as fact.

Love has been a sticky issue for us in previous times, but now, much to my immense gratification, it is an emotion directed at and shared by, each other. I love her with all my soul and would never do anything to hurt her…except…

Most of us spend our lives striving to make our parents proud. I can assure you; proud will not be the word on the tip of my mothers' tongue when she reads this book. Hell, it isn't something to be proud of, but it is the truth!

And that's what motivated me to write this book. As they say, if only one person gains from my loss, I will have fulfilled my duty. Maybe someone will recognize a similar behavioral pattern. Perhaps you know a person who suffers from expansive mood swings not unlike my own. In the book, I have provided a list of symptoms required to meet the DSM-IV R criteria for Bipolar Affective Disorder, or manic depression,but I think sometimes people have a hard time taking short, impersonal statements and applying them to their own experiences. I suspect some might find it easier to relate to specific situations. If you recognize yourself in my story, I urge you to take action and not incur anymore waste or damage to your life.

It's time to stop self-medicating with drugs or alcohol. It is also important to understand that certain forms of depression cannot be overcome by self-help regiments either, they need medical evaluation and treatment. For me, the only twelve steps I wanted to take when I was sick were the ones that got me behind the door to my bedroom.

Depression and manic depression are like other illnesses that people can have without being aware of its presence. They may chalk it up to "having a dark side", or just plain "being a bitch". That would explain why it frequently goes untreated. Or, if they do realize they are suffering from a mental illness, they believe it is a punishment for being a bad person. It is not!

What it is, is a debilitating illness with a physical cause - like diabetes, heart disease or arthritis. Essentially, it is a chemical imbalance, which causes a disturbance in brain chemistry, resulting in mood disorders. If you think a family member or friend has manic depression, it is just as important for you to read this book, because it is very hard to imagine what a person goes through if they have not experienced the wretchedness of this illness themselves. My own diagnosis of manic depression has set off the phenomenon by which you become highly aware of things you hadn't noticed before. For example, if you've ever had a pregnancy scare, while you're still unsure whether you are or not, all of a sudden you see pregnant women and babies everywhere you go. Since I was diagnosed with a mood disorder, I have come in contact with many people who either are already on psychiatric medication or speculate that they might have a problem in that area. I thought, this had for to be more than a coincidence, it must be a "sign". And as the manic-depressive motto goes: Don't Ignore the Signs! *Here is my story.*

...For most of my life I have gone through extensive periods of living in a "fog". This fog was much like bad television reception; it was irritating and hard to define the true picture. At times it got so thick it choked my perception of reality. In public, I would suffer this deep, anguishing haze, under a mask of, what I hoped would pass as, normalcy. In private, I succumbed to the tears and sheer physical pain while holding myself hostage in my room for as long as I could. When the fog dissipated, after a few weeks or months, it was soon followed by what I would describe as a hyper-clarity. Life became too bright, too loud to be easily absorbed. I became too bright, too loud, too busy to be believed. These episodes had considerable impact on my life, to say the least, and I found myself wishing, time and time again, that there was a pill I could take that would straighten things out - put some balance in my life and above all make me stop acting the way I did sometimes.

Completely unaware of manic depressive illness, I had no idea how prophetic these longings were to be...

Chapter One: Now

At least two or three times a year, my daughter, who is nine, will ask me what my favorite season of the year is. Without hesitation I tell her it's Fall. I am forever entranced with that spectacular season because of the explosions of colour garnishing the trees, warm afternoons and the way the air smells slightly wintery towards the dinner hour. I always feel renewed at this time of year…a new school year…new school clothes…a new pattern to the day. Back to the good old days of routine. I am most definitely what you would call, a creature of habit. So when the fall of '95 came around and I didn't have that "autumnal enthusiasm", I was a bit surprised. This time my usual sense of anticipation was intercepted by a foreboding feeling and I had no idea what the source of this discontentment was. There were no external reasons to which I could attribute.

My husband and I had the good fortune of buying our first new home in the spring and I was completely happy getting family and furniture settled in over the summer months. As a matter of fact, the previous 10 months were pretty good. I'd had some down times, but more than not, I'd snap out of them within a few days…a week - tops. I wouldn't get too concerned because you see, I was still on my antidepressants and things wouldn't really get THAT bad! Not like the old days, anyway. Although, I must admit at times things did get a bit out of hand and I would instinctively reach for the phone to make an appointment with Dr. Ryder. More often than not I ended up cancelling, just prior to, because…hey…I was feeling better now, so what was the point? Needless to say that wasn't the smart thing to do. And that foreboding feeling? It should have been my wake-up call.

Toward the end of October I started to feel run-down. Going to the gym was taking more effort than usual. For the past year or so, working out was one of the things I looked forward to most during the week. I was in better shape than I had ever been in my life and it was something I enjoyed maintaining...besides I could get my young son Noah out of my hair for ninety glorious minutes, three times a week! Cardiovascular fitness... forget it. I was striving for a little quiet time. Easily, I began to find reasons to drop a workout here and there. I was just too tired; I had so much to do... I was feeling overwhelmed lately. I was not getting things done around the house as quickly and efficiently as I normally would and I seemed to run on a very short fuse. Noises the kids normally made now seared through my head like hot needles and my reactive screaming felt like those needles were being pulled out the other side. I was also feeling bruised by the aches and pains that pummeled my body. For the life of me I didn't know why I was in such bad shape. Creating even more confusion, I would enjoy a good day now and then. On one such day, in a burst of energy, I went to the local nursery and bought a large paper bag of red Darwin Tulips and huge yellow headed King Alfred Daffodil bulbs. I was in such high spirits I treated myself (and my garden) to the purchase of a French Presidential lilac bush. When I got home, I got down and dirty in the garden until I had buried half of the bulbs in the back garden and positioned the lilac bush in its spot under the kitchen window. I envisioned, after a few years of forced patience, when it was ripe and ready, the deep mauve blossoms sharing their happy heady scent to those at the breakfast table.

But that's as far as I got. In the days following I began to descend into my own deep hole.

Now it was dawning on me that there was something definitely wrong...and it wasn't simply the flu. Finally, I made another appointment with my doctor...and this time I kept it.

I told her that I'd been going up and down for the past year, but now the downs were coming more frequently and getting harder and harder to transcend. I also had my manic episodes, but truth be told, they were a bit of a blessing. They got me up and doing the things I needed to get done. And besides, I would only get hypo-manic, which is a milder form of mania. I wasn't out buying Lear jets and five thousand-dollar outfits! When I wondered if my medication was working anymore, she suggested I try a mood stabilizer such as Lithium along with my Desipramine, to help smooth things out. She explained that antidepressants are great for getting a manic-depressive out of a depression but they don't always

14

maintain balance. In fact, they can send you right into a manic episode. A mood stabilizer, like Lithium, which can also be effective in some cases of depression, helps stabilize someone who is in a manic state. Lithium won't cure manic depression...it can prevent or reduce the frequency and severity of future mood-swings. Well, this information fell on deaf ears. LITHIUM! Ohmigod...LITHIUM! There is no way I was going to turn myself into a 40 lb. - heavier version of myself...someone who couldn't even get a cup of coffee to her lips without losing half of it into her lap! Uh-uh, give me a new antidepressant!

Dr. Ryder straightened me out on the Lithium issue, then patiently explained my other options, including some of the newer antidepressants that work differently than the one I was presently on. I will discuss more about the biology of depression and other treatments that are available in a later chapter.

I must say here, that not only was, and is, Dr. Ryder a concerned and caring doctor, she provided me with all the information I needed (sometimes over and over again - until I got it) to help me choose the path I would take to wellness.

I always felt whatever my choice was, I had her full support and guidance. After some deliberation, I decided to ditch my Desipramine and try a new antidepressant on the market called Manerix.

When going off of one antidepressant medication, you must observe what is called a "wash-out" period before starting a new one. Your doctor will let you know what the recommended time is depending on the medications involved. I was to taper off the Desipramine over a few days, "wash-out" for a week and then start on the Manerix. I was very excited about this new drug because it was touted as having very few side-affects. Desipramine was causing me constipation, twitches and dry-mouth, which is the kiss of death to someone in the broadcasting industry! Manerix was also said to not cause sexual dysfunction. YIPPEE! (That was my husband). Things were pretty dry in that department too! We had not had a very healthy sex life for the past year or so.

Two days after I began to taper my Desipramine I became very ill. I was completely immobile. I lay in bed suffering horrible headaches, sleeping away the days and at night, woke up over and over from the chill of cold sweats. I was a mess. I continually cried and rarely ate a thing.

I obsessed about the state I was in and was totally blown away by the smallest of issues. When Stephen couldn't get home early to take over, all I could manage to do around the house was the bare minimum: Feed the kids. And believe me, Betty Crocker and Kraft get all the credit for those "meals".

When Stephen was home then I would officially hide out under a big, wet, black woollen blanket of misery. I figured I must have caught a cold or flu (although sometimes when a patient goes off an antidepressant they will experience flu-like symptoms) and then had a major bout of depression descend upon me. And on top of it all ...my in-laws came for a visit! I would haul my scraggy head down the stairs when they came to visit the kids and within twenty minutes, I'd be bawling my eyes out for no apparent reason! I'm sure they had some very interesting conversations on the car ride home about their son's safety! If only he had married... (insert name of other worthy woman)!

Twice, during this crisis, I managed to pull myself together; once to produce the radio talk show I worked on part-time, which was being broadcast from Ottawa that night. I must have flipped over into a manic-mode because, never having produced a remote show before, I managed dealing with the operator, here in Vancouver, the other producer and host in Ottawa, and screened no less than a hundred calls from across Canada. If a 747 had of pulled up in front of the station windows that night... I could'a landed that baby... no sweat! Of course I was the one that crashed as soon as I got home after the show. The other occasion was my husband's grandmother's 80th birthday party, which the entire family flew in to celebrate. I made it to the nearest mall and got my hair coloured (the gray was growing in with a vengeance), went on a bit of a shopping spree and showed up at the party later that night looking not bad at all, under the circumstances, if I may say so myself. Thank-you Maybelline! Carefully concealed was the fact that I was going through one of the most desperate times of my life. And despite the new medication, not counting the cranium-crushing headaches I was developing, nothing much had changed.

We tried increasing the dosage again, but all it did was cause problems getting to sleep. When I finally managed to nod off, I had dreams that would've made Jeffry Dalhmer cringe in fright! And the night-

16

sweats...wow!

Waking up in the middle of the night drenched in sweat but freezing at the same time, has got to be one of the most uncomfortable sensations I've ever experienced. So finally after 6 weeks on Manerix, Dr. Ryder convinced me that we had tried long enough and it was time to face the fact that this particular medication just wasn't working for me. I stayed on Manerix for so long because, although I had felt relief on my first medication (when I was initially diagnosed with depression) within 2 weeks, I knew that it usually takes between 4 and 6 weeks for symptoms to start to subside. Once again, Dr. Ryder suggested that I also take a small dose of Lithium daily to increase the effect of the Manerix, but again I balked at the thought of going on Lithium.

I had no reason for feeling this way. I guess maybe I felt Lithium had some stigma attached to it. Funny, thinking back, that the word "lithium" scared me, yet I was fine with the term "manic depression".

After going through what I call the "antidepressant drive-thru menu" (I believe there are at least 20 different medications) I decided to try the Selective Serotonin Reuptake Inhibitor (SSRI) category. Paxil, the brand name for the drug paroxetine, was the one we felt would be appropriate for me to try at this stage. You've probably heard of another popular medication in this group called Prozac (fluoxetine) or Zoloft (sertraline). Paxil was the one least likely to have an agitating effect out of the three, which was what I needed considering my tendency toward hypo-manic episodes. Welbutrin (bupropion) is another second-generation antidepressant that is known to be a good medication for the patient with a tendency toward mania and rapid cycling (at least four distinctive mood swings within a year). But Welbutrin also has the side effect of causing a loss of appetite. People who are already underweight should probably not take this drug. Considering I had a history of eating disorders, we decided against this one too. As I went through the washout period between medications again, I found myself in a "mixed-state"; this is when you have both manic and depressive symptoms at the same time.

You are so agitated that it feels like every cell in your body is buzzing. You're about to explode because your heart is lodged in your throat, slam dancing with your esophagus and at the same time, you cannot move a muscle. Body and mind are leaden. The thought of the house burning

17

down around you is comforting because you just can't seem to get warm enough anyway.

At one point I started to feel particularly discouraged. Was I ever well? I couldn't remember anymore. Would I get better or was this it from here on in? Oh please God... I'm not one of those people they call "unresponsives", am I? Dr. Ryder had to remind me that, yes, I had done very well for a long time and my chances of recovery again were very good.

Soon my son would be turning three and I had made it through some of the toughest times in a parent's life.

Though by the skin of my teeth!

Since Noah's birth, I had pictured myself approaching his third birthday feeling rather triumphant in having survived Baby Boot Camp and confident of the freedom at hand. Being a parent is one of, if not the hardest things a person can do, and not to minimize anyone's parental endeavors, I believe it to be even harder for someone with a mood disorder. But more on that topic later.

On January 1st, 1996, I rang in the New Year by taking my 1st dose of Paxil with my morning coffee and toast. I started on half the regular dosage (half of a 20mg pill) for a week and then went up to the full 20 mg's. Through out the month, I went to see Dr. Ryder once a week to talk about how things were going. I didn't respond to Paxil as quickly as I did to Desipramine either, but I wasn't panicking yet. I knew I needed to give it time. One thing that did bother me was whether I would recognize when and if I was feeling better.

Except for enjoying better sleep patterns, usually it is a family member or friend who notices the changes first, especially in a severely depressed person. A person may say that they're feeling better, but are they doing the things they did when they were well? Are they spending time in their garden? Are they interested in their hobbies again? Are they getting pleasure from watching or playing their favourite sport? For me it is reading. When I'm depressed, I can barely read the TV guide, and yet when I'm well, I read close to a book a week. Your family and friends are the ones who can more objectively see if you are responding to treatment, if you are becoming more balanced. They notice that you are not as irritable or hostile and that warmth and affection is responded to and even reciprocated. They can see you start to live again. But of course, most importantly, it is you that needs to know where you stand. You need to see the progress you're making, if in fact, you are making progress.

Something that really helped me put things into perspective was the Beck Depression Inventory. This is a simple self-rating scale questionnaire that Dr. Ryder instructed me to fill out once a week. Through a group of questions you're asked to describe how you feel using a selection of degrees from 0 to 3; for example:

0   I do not feel sad.
1   I feel sad.
2   I am sad all the time and I can't snap out of it.
3   I am so sad or unhappy that I can't stand it.

You answer the question by choosing the statement that defines how you have felt over the last week, including that day. You can also use more that one statement if it so fits. I filled out the questionnaire once a week and brought it to my doctor's appointments. She tallied the scores up and showed me how things were going. I remember one of the questions in the test had to do with your ability to make decisions. I found it amusing that I couldn't always answer this one because I was having problems deciding whether I was having problems making a decision. That pretty much said it all right there. These questionnaires are also useful for someone who is on a fixed dosage of medication, but suspects that there is something wrong because they are experiencing breakthrough symptoms, such as having problems with sleep patterns again. Their dosage might need to be changed because of physical illness or stressful personal experiences.

Eventually, after 3 or 4 weeks I did start to feel better, calmer inside and out. I had more energy to do things around the house and could handle the kids better.

The meals still weren't Grade A, but believe me, no one was complaining! I would have some bad days but not as many and not nearly as devastating. I must tell you though, I did insulate myself on those bad days by taking a 1/2 of a .5 mg Ativan once or twice a day, as needed. This is about 1/6th of a normal daily dose for someone suffering from anxiety, so I didn't feel too guilty, and besides, the important thing was that everyone was alive at the end of the day.

When someone is in a hypo-manic state, a tranquilizer, such as Ativan, helps take the edge off. It didn't sedate me really, it just brought me down to a normal level and helped me cope.

Having said that, Dr. Ryder would have to "give me permission" to use this sort of relief, because I felt so weak, so guilty, for taking a tranquilizer. Only "three times divorced, 3 o'clock in the afternoon martini-tipping, Hollywood Wives" took tranq's, right? So I used Ativan on three or four occasions until the antidepressant truly kicked-in and the extreme anxiety went away.

As far as side effects from this particular antidepressant were concerned, the ones I dealt with at the outset were headaches, agitation, disrupted sleep patterns, constipation and sleepiness. I now take half my pill in the morning and the other half in the early evening, which seems to help with the drowsiness problem, although I do find that I still need to take a nap in the afternoon. But then I've needed a daily nap for as long as I can remember. I guess I just need more rest than most to function properly. Maybe I should move to Spain, where the siesta is a normal part of one's day. Now that I think about it, getting enough sleep seems to be a buffer against mood swings, at least for me it is. In the evening, I take a natural bulk-laxative to keep things running smoothly, so to speak, and other than some fatigue and the occasional headache, I am happy and healthy. I can hardly believe I am able to say that now.

After about 6 or 7 weeks on Paxil, I started to feel a sort of rebirth, a re-entry into the land of the living.

Coincidentally, but symbolically, I think, my daffodils made their appearance at the same time.

Chapter Two: Then

I wouldn't describe myself as a "depressed" child, as a matter of fact, I don't think I would describe myself as any particular kind of child because I don't remember much of that part of my life. Until the age of twelve or thirteen my memories are reluctantly retrieved from a gray area. Of course, I can call up a few warm, fuzzy or tribulant moments. But for the most part, my reflections are marred by uncertainty. My mother, however is quite clear when she says, when questioned, that they had no problems with me at all. I behaved as well as any other kid, at home and at school. I had many friends and pretty much did what I was told. Although, she said, I did harbor a great desire to be an only child, as I didn't appreciate the presence of my sisters very much. This fact I was surprised to hear, because I don't recall feeling that way. But I can confirm, however, that my mother and I had many difficult moments. What they were about I'm not so sure, but we did lock horns frequently. She said that I wasn't exactly a happy child, and my Dad and her weren't sure what to do about it. In retrospect, I imagine, my mother found it strenuous trying to deal with three other daughters and keep me reasonably content with life. I think I blamed her, in my childish way, for not being able to accomplish the task. I was never convinced of my mother's love. Although she may think that my chronic unhappiness as a child is inconsequential in regards to my illness now, I think it is substantial. I don't remember specific reasons for it, but I also felt an encompassing loneliness.

But, as my mother said, I had no shortage of playmates, so this sense of isolation was something that my parents, friends and relatives, would be confused to hear about. And the contradiction was that, while I felt lonely, I very much wanted to be left alone.

I believe my depressions started around the summer of my thirteenth birthday. I was invited to spend a couple of weeks at my aunt's house in a small town in Ontario. She had a pretty little white trimmed brick house with a lush, tree-lined back yard for her three small children to play in. Across the street lived a family with three young girls whom my sisters and I had made friends with on previous summer vacations. There was a community swimming pool down the road to cool off in and a convenience store where we spent every penny we had on Slush Puppies and Icy Cups. My aunt was very special to my older sister and myself when we were very young. After my mother and her first husband, my biological father, divorced, she was always doing special things for us. When she married, we were made a part of the wedding (Marlo Thomas "That Girl" hair-dos and all) and we were happy to see our new uncle join the family. Sometimes my aunt would throw a party in my honour when my birthday coincided with our holiday. I was secretly thrilled to see my winterborn sisters glare at me with eyes green with envy. So when, this particular summer, I was invited without my sisters for a visit, I was over the moon! But all did not go as I, and I'm sure my aunt, had anticipated. Not long after my arrival, I became frustrated and annoyed at having my young cousins around all the time (I don't know what else I could have expected) and I really resented being asked to help out by folding laundry or keeping an eye on one of the kids for a minute or two.

My aunt is a vivacious, get-up-and-go type of person... a real believer in "lots of fresh air" and all I really wanted to do that summer was to sleep in late, lie on the couch and watch TV, or take naps - basically to be left alone! I guess I should have gone to Palm Springs! Being 13 years old, this attitude could have been attributed to a "hormone" thing, but the lethargy and hostility I felt was really intense. I think I have always been emotionally sensitive. If I liked... I really liked... if I hated... I really hated... and when I felt sad and alone in the world... well you get the idea. A few years earlier, when we lived in Saskatchewan, there was an undeveloped area behind our townhouse complex (I guess they could have been called "prairies") where during the summer holidays I would pitch a small tent with rocks, sticks and an old blanket, lay on the parched ground inside and wish that I never had to go back home. I would lay there just listening to the wind whirling around me. And though the consolation I felt in this seclusion was great, thoughts of rabid prairie dogs

22

and thorny tumbleweeds would inevitably send me home.

Getting back to my holiday, it turned out to be a real fiasco and I was actually happy to see my sisters and parents when they arrived at my aunt's house later on that month. Evidently my mother and grandmother had spent some time discussing my unhappy demeanor during their summer visit on the East Coast and came up with the idea of suggesting to me that I go to live with my grandmother in St. John's, Newfoundland. I'm quite sure neither of them had really expected me to take them up on the offer, so when I agreed to make the big move, only next year, after my last year of junior high, they were astonished!

My mother thought even though I insisted I would go through with the move, I would change my mind before the year was out. But I didn't. I don't know where the motivation for leaving my family came from, but all I thought about during those twelve months was the fact that I was going! It wasn't as though I had to escape from a bad situation.

I had as normal a family as anyone else can testify to. My mother got a little stressed out and shrill at times but who wouldn't with four kids to care for, two teens and two under seven! My father, a Canadian Air Force pilot, was away for long periods of time and that added to the burden. Knowing what I know now, I think my mother might have had her own struggles with depression during those difficult years.

When the next summer came around, we all flew to Newfoundland with one less person being on the flight back. My mother was convinced that I would be back home within weeks, and was shocked as months went by without word from me wanting to return. This was the child that a couple of years earlier declined summer camp for fear of being homesick.

At the beginning of the school year I was enrolled in a Catholic all-girls high school and had no problem at all adjusting to my new life. I made friends and was quickly one of the "in-crowd". Depending on who you were and how you looked at it, that was either a good or bad accomplishment.

Before the end of grade nine, I was smoking cigarettes (back then that was a big deal) and not long into grade ten, I graduated to smoking pot and drinking on a regular basis.

I discovered that the inner agitation I often struggled with was quelled by these vices. My grandmother and her husband both worked full time and had no idea what was going on in my life. He was a brewery employee with an alcohol problem and when he brought his work home with him, so to speak, he became an unsuspecting contributor to my own alcohol abuse. I became increasingly self-centered and intent on doing what I wanted, when I wanted, despite the consequences. My behavior was, to say the least, reckless; quite often I hitchhiked, with friends or alone, drunk or sober. On more than one occasion I found myself in potentially dangerous situations, but nothing was going to stop me from getting to where I wanted to go, figuratively or literally. I began to stay out way past my curfew on both school and weekend nights and a few times actually slept outside or in a friend's car while I was thought to be safe and sound at a schoolmate's house.

Essentially, my teen years were filled with drinking, smoking, doing drugs, and shoplifting clothing and cheap jewelry to wear to the endless parties I was bent on attending. I laugh (sort of) now, when I say that, yes, I went to university - to every beer bash that was thrown between '77 and '80!

Unfortunately, what I wasn't interested in attending was high school. Towards the end, I wasn't there much and didn't care at all. For many years I have felt incredible guilt over this behavior, especially since my parents and grandmother were unaware that I was so out of control. One explanation of this "acting out" could be that I was just a troubled kid looking for love and acceptance. The problem with that theory is that I was never in want of friends, I was always very popular with my peers, and had my share of boyfriends, too. Although, I must say, my first experience with love was rather fervent. I was completely destroyed when my first boyfriend went off to the navy, and I lived only to check the mail for his letters. He was all I thought about. All I cared about. This state of mourning went on for almost a year when someone or something else suddenly distracted me, wiping out any trace of the deep sadness that had consumed me for so long.

When I got something in my head, be it a party, an outfit or boyfriend, that was all that existed. I became completely obsessed and wouldn't rest until I had satiated the need. The problem with getting what I wanted was that, not long after, I would pivot into some other preoccupation. And there was another side to this erratic behavior. It was one of disinterest and lethargy. I would not want to become involved in activities that normally intrigued me. I would go straight home after school and sleep for hours in front of the TV, with my head bowed over the arm of the chair, occasionally waking up to shift to the other side. My grandmother's husband would crack open his inebriated eye (the other was glass) and "harumpf" in disgust at my laziness and fall back into his own unconsciousness on the couch of many-cigarette-burns, across from me.

During these "down times", I felt I could not get enough sleep, no matter when I went to bed. I frequently dozed through class at school and complained that the fluorescent lighting made me feel like dead weight. It was as if I was losing my very self somehow - like a slow leak in a tire. I drank and did drugs through out these periods, hoping they would energize me back to my "normal" self.

The teenage years are all about figuring out who you are, and for me, just when I thought I had the answer, the equation would change. I would have new friends, new interests, new boyfriends and new jobs. And there's nothing wrong with that... when you're a teenager. No one expects much in the way of stability from you in those years.

As I got older, I found that things weren't as simple... and people weren't as forgiving.

Insights on Manic Depressive Illness: Childhood

• The biggest obstacle a child with a mood disorder is up against, is recognition and acknowledgment of the illness from their parents or even family doctors. Too easily are children's behavioral problems written off as just that - they're bad, lazy, incorrigible kids. Only since the early 80's has it been accepted by the medical profession that children do indeed, suffer from depressive illnesses. Like adults, children can suffer from many types of psychiatric problems including, eating and panic disorders, tourette's syndrome, depression and manic depression. If the child's family history is one that includes members with depressive illness, substance and/or alcohol abuse, there is an even greater chance that the child is or will suffer a depressive or manic episode. These psychiatric disorders will most likely become apparent through difficulties with social, school, friend and family relationships.

• Kids and adolescents who regularly consume drugs and alcohol are not necessarily just bored or delinquent. If they have an undiagnosed mood disorder, most likely they are self-medicating and this will inevitably make matters worse for them.

• Symptoms of juvenile manic depression are:
   - cycling moods with intense emotions such as anger, aggression and irritability, or, elevated, silly, over-talkative behavior.
   - feelings of hopelessness and sadness, loss of interest in hobbies.
   - thoughts of death or suicide.
   - hyperactive level of energy or chronic lack of energy.
   - school problems such as: phobia about attending, anxiety over homework or tests, lack of concentration distractability, fatique or peer problems tired peer problems.* Although some children can still do well in school while suffering from depression
      - drug and/or alcohol abuse
      - impulsivity, shoplifting
      - early and vigorous sexual activity

• Many children with manic depression are misdiagnosed as schizo-phrenic because of their agitated, expansive behavior. They have also been diagnosed with Attention Deficit Disorder when they present low levels of concentration and high levels of energy.

• Once a child experiences an episode of major depression, it is very like-ly that he or she will have another in the future.

• Medical treatment of manic depression in juveniles is found to be high-ly effective. In fact if it is not treated, symptoms can become more severe causing further behavioral problems and potential suicide attempts.

Chapter Three: Love and Marriage

I was recently reunited with one of my best friends from my adolescence after losing contact with her for more than 16 years. We went to the same Catholic high school and were roommates for a while before I moved to the other side of the country where time and distance eventually disconnected us. One particularly "down" evening, coasting on a wave of nostalgia, I discovered through a couple of long distance phone calls, that she was living less than a hundred miles away from me in a small suburb of Victoria, on Vancouver Island. A month later, after many long distance phone calls, I took the ferry over to the island and spent a weekend getting reacquainted. We shared embarrassing old pictures and love letters that had been concealed from any beholder for over a decade, a bottle of wine and laughed till we couldn't anymore, as we went through all three. I told her about my diagnosis of bipolar disorder and she looked as though she had had a profound revelation. Way back when we were living together, she admitted, there were times when my behavior had completely baffled her. I would spend days alone in my sparse room sleeping on the mattress on the floor, totally uncommunicative with the outside world and then literally burst out of my seclusion declaring that life was one big party and I was invited. She said she never quite knew how to approach me, I was either remote or rejoicing, without rhyme or reason. There had to be some near normal times because I did manage to hold down a job without many problems.

Actually, I held down many jobs, not all at the same time, one after another, after another! Skip... to... my... Lou...

My love life was a turbulent reflection of my many moods. I would establish a relationship that would go through the normal ups and downs and then, out of the blue, after being together for a few months, sometimes as long as a couple of years, I would wake up one morning and decide "Hey, this isn't for me... I'm outta here!" I swear I would literally wake up a different person and change my life accordingly. After one such "awakening", I dumped a boyfriend of two years, immediately initiated a reunion with my first boyfriend and a month into that relationship, decided to move out west to Alberta. My plans were to live with my sister in Fort McMurray, a northern oil-boom community, make money, hand-over-fist, in the hotel business, and then, when the time was right, send word for my boyfriend to join me. Just a minor change of pace!

But the time never was right for our reconnection. I quickly changed my mind, again, after I settled in my latest place of residence and decided that my "new" boyfriend wouldn't fit into my "new" life. I must admit, though, many others did! I circulated through a revolving door of relationships for the next couple of years. A lot of them being very intense at the outset and then suddenly snuffed out by indifference. More than once I had become involved with guys that were completely unsuitable, I mean, they were the polar opposite of what I had ever needed , wanted or even liked for that matter! But as usual, those guys never lasted long either. How any of them survived my arbitrary moods for more than a few weeks is beyond me and I am sure a few sighed in relief when I vacated their lives.

Something that was of resilience in this small town was its big city vices, a constant supply of high-grade drugs and alcohol. Because I worked in hotel nightclubs and pubs, I was always around or involved with some kind of substance abuse situation. We partied before, on and after the job. In this bitterly cold community of people with more money than they knew what to do with... that was what we did. And for someone who went through manic phases, this was as close to Nirvana as I was going to get. The knowledge that employees were under the influence was easily swallowed by management. In fact, many played host to the internal party. I remember one of my bosses setting up a few lines of cocaine in the back room to help us get started on our shift. I also remember that many of those shifts began at 11 a.m.!

Strangely enough, as many times as I found myself insatiable to the effects of drugs and alcohol, I never once felt myself addicted to either. The lure of some substances quickly wore off as I became familiar with their effects. The more cocaine I did, the less I liked it. If I was depressed, it made me a "paranoid" depressive who couldn't stop talking about how bad things were, and if I was manic, it just agitated me to new heights. Subsequently, cocaine was not something I had a particularly hard time turning down; frankly, it wasn't worth the exertion. The experiences I had with LSD and other hallucinogens like magic mushrooms while I was in high school were similar and being squeamish in the presence of needles, heroin or any drug taken intravenously was not even considered not that it was even part of my realm anyway.

Ah... but the alcohol. When I was feeling down, drinking seemed to kill the pain or at least dull it for a while. I hoped the inebriation would help me feel more like "my old self". When I was up - good (hyper-happy)... well... for she's a jolly good fella! I couldn't help but celebrate how great both myself and life in general, was! When I was up - bad (agitated and hostile) a quick quaff was the only thing I could do to calm myself down and make me feel more balanced. Try and use that excuse at police stop-checks! Speaking of which, I am embarrassed and ashamed to admit that during the 70's it was no small miracle that I had never injured others or myself while driving under the influence... greatly under the influence.

And I was not alone. Being in the business I was, there was never a lack of company, so it didn't seen so dysfunctional. Everyone was doing it! There were times, though, when I didn't indulge in any form of intoxicator. I just didn't have the taste for it. Or maybe I didn't have the need. I suppose I must have been enjoying some sense of equilibrium during those phases. Regrettably that's just what they were, phases, mitigating, never enduring.

I was in yet another relationship that wasn't going so great, when, one day I started crying. After two weeks, I still hadn't stopped. I was so depressed I couldn't climb out of bed or eat and phoned in sick at work as often as I could, without risk of being fired. When I did make my shift, the mask I wore to hide my true feelings took so much effort to maintain, I was completely sapped of energy by the time I clocked out. I never showed up at any of the parties held after-hours and had only the occasional drink at home. I started to lose weight and became concerned that there might be something physically wrong with me. I finally went to a doctor and with a couple of pats on the head, he sent me off with a prescription in hand.

I'm not a hundred percent sure, but I believe it was for Elavil. This was

31

the first antidepressant I had ever taken. But I had no idea what it was or what it was for. For some reason the doctor neglected to let me in on that pertinent piece of information. After a week on this medication I did stop crying but I also stopped laughing and smiling. I was as responsive to my environment as a zombie. When I started having problems swallowing, I decided the side effects were worse than the symptoms and flushed them down the toilet.

One night not long after, I felt such inexplicable despair that I ingested a handful of asprin. I really don't know what I was attempting to do; I felt that I just couldn't go on the way I was without doing something, even something that pathetically impotent. Other than making me very nauseous and causing me to see things in duplicate, through a wash of yellow, nothing but a poor nights sleep was the result. Needless to say, an acetaminophen overdose can be very dangerous - don't try this!

Eventually I snapped out of this "mood" and life, as it was, went on.

I made excellent money on my shifts at the nightclub, so when I decided to join a friend on her trip to Europe, it took me only three weeks to come up with the funds, and off I flew to the other side of the world

We toured with my companion's friend in his Peugeot through Holland, Belgium, France, down to the south of Spain and took a brief trip over to Portugal where after two or three days, dumped the car and driver to take a miserably long bus ride to Calpe, on the east coast of Spain. We found the weather bleak and windy for the most part, so after a month we flew over to Israel and spent some time in Elat and Tel Aviv, where the promise of warmer weather was well kept. The girlfriend I traveled with was born, I believe in France and lived for some time in Belgium. Her flirtatious nature and familiarity with five languages enabled us to communicate in each country without too much difficulty. All the same, I found it very hard to adjust to the diverse cultures. I was terrified by the alpine routes through France and exasperated by the lethargic pace in Spain. In Portugal - our car was broken into as we checked into out hotel. More intimately though, the toilet facilities throughout the trip were contaminated at best. Flushing commodes, toilet tissue, paper towels and running water were considered perks.

I found Israel, on the other hand, to be a very comforting place, despite the casual attitude toward bearing arms. It was commonplace to see machineguns slung over the shoulders of shoppers looking for the perfect avocado. I enjoyed that particular leg of the trip immensely and pushed my return date to Belgium back two extra weeks. During my visit, I shakily maneuvered a jeep across the border into Egypt, snorkeled in the reefs of the Red Sea and baked topless on the hot smooth rocks of Rafi Nelson beach. Back in Elat, I mastered enough skills in windsurfing to get me within shouting distance of the war ships on alert in the harbor and within reach of the giant sea turtles, not to mention the sharks, which inhabit the waters.

Does this sound like the same person who could barely converse, a few months earlier? Hardly. I mourned my departure from Israel, feeling I was leaving a part of me behind. And in retrospect, I did, for I have never again experienced the sense of strength and fearlessness I did there. Even now, I will not swim in waters that are unchlorinated or deeper than my height.

Shortly after returning to Ft. McMurray I decided to move a bit south, to Edmonton, Alberta, with another boyfriend. During the summer and early autumn months, I worked outdoors as an industrial painter at an oil refinery, painting nuts, bolts and stretches of piping, scorching silver. When the temperatures dropped, I picked up a job at a popular country and western bar. I worked hard on the job and hard at home trying to ride the tide through another failing relationship. My moods were causing an irreparable amount of stress and made eating almost impossible for me. I lost a considerable amount of weight (including the excess I acquired on my European trip) but gained an empowerment I hadn't felt for a long time. Wielding this new strength, I took on another job, in addition to the waitressing at night. Now I was working eighteen to nineteen hours a day fortified by one piece of toast with peanut butter, sliced into four strips, and a glass of skim milk. I drank and did drugs to help ignore the hunger I was feeling. When I did have a weak moment and gave in to the need to eat, I would swallow increasing amounts of laxatives afterwards and endure the wracking spasms that would purge my body of the nutrients of which it had been so deprived.

I punished my body with this "power" for approximately two years and dropped to 90 lbs, before this irrational need, for some reason, gradually dissipated.

On a weekend trip further south, to Calgary, I had a love-at-first-site experience, regardless of the fact I was vacationing with my boyfriend of a couple of years. This new relationship was ignited by an extreme chemical attraction that compelled me to sever all personal and work ties and move to the area, permanently. In a rare reversal of roles, this new love extinguished our affair less than six months later. It wasn't easy, being the "dumpee", but I rebounded quickly. I spent much of my time with my new roommate, a girl I also worked with. We went to bars together and essentially did the single girl's routine. It was one of the few times I wasn't connected to some form of boyfriend. I was having a tremendous time and was so flattered by the male attention I was getting, I found it hard to turn down a date. After a few months of frantic socializing, I started to run out of steam and that's when my first husband stumbled into my life. I met him while I was on sick leave from a restaurant recovering from foot surgery. At the outset, I didn't think it was a union worth pursuing but, the more we saw of each other, the more grounded I felt. It was like I was coming down from a prolonged high. One that I was weary from. I came to the conclusion that what I was experiencing this time was a "mature" relationship; one based on a foundation of friendship not infatuation and insatiable lust. Within three months Edward and I moved in together. He worked in various restaurants while I went to school. Another round of agitation soon started up with depression lurking in the background. I was beginning to feel restless and distressed again, for no apparent reason.

At twenty-four years old, I calculated twenty-eight changes of residences in my life! Most of them were small moves within the same city. Still, it's no surprise I never felt "grounded". I got the idea that maybe the problem was that I was always the roommate... and never the bride. Thinking a legal certificate would give me a sense of permanence, I suggested we get married. Yeah... that's the ticket! Once the novelty of the engagement wore off, I realized that I wasn't feeling any better. Actually things were getting worse, but by then I attributed it to "cold feet". The feelings of doom continued, yet I persisted with the wedding plans. With the help of half a magnum of champagne and half a Valium, I floated down the aisle to wedded bliss. You've heard the expression "it was no honeymoon", well, it wasn't. We fought down the coast of California and back. Of course, things didn't improve when we got home. But, hey, I had an idea!! Let's move!! It's always worked before - right?! This time it was to Vancouver, British Columbia. We had passed through on our way back from our honeymoon and were quite taken with its incredible mountainous coastline. It was exciting settling in to this fair city. I felt buoyed by its energy despite the relentless rain during the winter months. Eventually I landed a job at one of the nicer hotels downtown. I earned a good union wage topped off nicely by tips from a generous clientele. Things were finally going smoothly. Just as I was tempted to write off my previous unhappiness to not living in the right place, depression set in again and this time I decided the resolution would be to become a parent! You know... a baby will bring us closer... will seal the circle... make us a family!

This was probably one of the only delusions I suffered.

Insights on Manic Depressive Illness

• According to one study, nearly half of women with alcohol abuse problems are seriously depressed and that most of them have had depressive episodes before the actual abuse began. Because the depression goes unrecognized, therefore, untreated, these women tend to relapse after periods of sobriety.

• Some people with manic depressive illness drink to ease their anxieties, while others may look to cocaine to help their struggles with depression. Cocaine is sometimes used by the person experiencing a manic episode who feels invincible and never wants to "come down". Alcohol and cocaine raise neurotransmitter levels in the brain causing people with depressive illness to self-medicate because these substances actually make them feel better. They are searching for the physical and mental balance that others, who are not suffering from chemical deficiencies, seem to have. Unfortunately the "balance" they achieve through these substances is only temporary and puts them in further jeopardy by adding addiction to their problems.

• Studies show that nearly half of women with bulimia have suffered a depressive episode before their eating disorder appeared.

• Eating disorders, such as bulimia and anorexia, are not necessarily caused by family or social background - they are also linked to neurochemical changes in the brain. Research has found that there is a connection between eating disorders and serotonin levels.

• Extreme dieting tends to elevate levels of natural morphine-like chemicals found in the brain called opiods. This creates a sort of "high" which reinforces the behavior. At the same time, starving oneself wreaks havoc on brain chemicals, especially the lowering of serotonin levels.

• Chemical imbalances that cause these eating disorders further punish the sufferer with distorted thoughts on food, eating, self image and weight.

• Bulimia is related to Obsessive Compulsive Disorder in that the bulimic is obsessed with thoughts of food, its caloric content, weight and clothing sizes. They repetitively measure their bodies and "weigh-in".

Some, though, will not go near a scale out of fear that they have gained weight. After they "give in" to the urge to binge on food, or just to eat a regular meal, the extreme guilt they feel compels them to purge the meal from their bodies by either vomiting or inflicting large amounts of laxatives on their systems. Intense exercise is a way some bulimics try to burn up calories they have just consumed. And then some rely on a combination of all of the above techniques to keep weight off.

• Just as untreated depression and mania can mysteriously go into remission, so can eating disorders, but they will most likely reappear, usually during periods of high stress.

• Frequently associated with alcoholism, depression, manic depression and eating disorders is Kleptomania. This is an illness in which the sufferer is compelled to steal. Items stolen are usually not things that are necessities. Every day, people turn off the urge to do things that are harmful to themselves and others or just plain inappropriate, by using what is called Voluntary Impulse Control. People who suffer from Bulimia, OCD and Kleptomania are said to be suffering from a disturbance in that particular nerve grouping in the brain. As a result, these people are unable to ignore or turn off urges to, count, wash hands, steal or other negative behavioral impulses. However, I am not suggesting that all people who shoplift are kleptomaniacs.

• Antidepressants that affect levels of the neurotransmitter Serotonin have shown some success in treating Kleptomania, as Serotonin affects mood, appetite and impulsivity.

**After reading the information above, it is important to remember that in people suffering from addictions to drugs and/or alcohol, a "mood disorder" could most likely be the "primary illness". It is also important to realize that self-help groups like Alcoholics Anonymous tend to discourage any association between addictions and psychiatric disorder.

Members who don't experience profound positive changes in their lives after sobriety are seen as failures. At one time, some of these groups actually equated antidepressants to "street drugs", although this was never said to be their "official" position. Nowadays self-help groups are more accepting of these medications than in the past.

Chapter Four: Baby

Ten minutes after I made the major life decision to become pregnant... I was. Throughout the nine months, Edward worked in the position he inherited from me at the hotel and spent substantial amounts of his time off in a rented garage working on cars. I was on my own a lot and when the down times hit, they packed a punch. The days slipped by me as I recoiled from my life in my bed, crying hysterically off and on, not bothering to get up to turn on the lights as the day slipped into the dark of evening. I was angry at my isolation, at my pregnancy, at my shell of a marriage, at our finances and that The Young and the Restless was preempted! Let me remind you, I still didn't know that I actually had a medically recognized mood disorder. I thought it was just me being the screwed-up, hateful, unhappy bitch I could sometimes be. The only alternative to that theory was that everyone around me was taking it on as a personal project to make my life hell. The addition of pregnancy hormones accelerated my paranoid rage like fuel sprayed on fire.

I would have to say that for most of my pregnancy with my first child, my daughter, I was in a pronounced depression and this was not alleviated by birth. Quite the opposite, it became deeper, darker and possibly dangerous.

When Noël was born, I felt only what I could describe as "shell-shock". The actual labor was long and very, very painful. Although I was prepared intellectually for the big event, for example, I knew that this baby was going to come out of that very small opening after a certain amount of torment and time, when it was actually happening, my mind was screaming. **OHMYGODTHISBABYISGOINGTOCOMEOUTOF... OHMYGODOHMYGODMAKEITSTOPMAKEITSTOP!!!!**

I knew the best thing I could do would be to give in and just let the process happen, but the pain and panic was overwhelming and I fought against the inevitable the whole way. After 17 hours of labor, my lovely light-weight daughter won the fight and I lurched off the delivery table and waddled down the hall looking for a shower to wash away the humiliation I felt over not handling the situation very well.

The hospital was a teaching hospital that held the philosophy of helping new mothers bond with their babies by having then stay in the same room 24 hours a day. Nurses would stop by frequently to make sure things were going smoothly. And though it was exactly the kind of arrangement I planned for myself and my baby, frankly, every time I heard them wheeling her back to my room after one routine test or another, my body would freeze with icy dread.

I had no idea how I was to look after this tiny ball of flesh and it stunned me that the nurses could obliviously place this child in my ignorant unsupervised care! The only person who sensed my discomposure was the lady who came in to vacuum the floors. She was kind enough to put down her hose to help me with my own suction problems as I tried to nurse my baby.

At night when family visitors had drifted home and staff was down to a bare minimum, I would jam my head in my pillow and sob over my incompetence. Maybe I would handle things better at home, I thought, so I asked to be released. Dumb... Dumb... Dumb! The same crushing apprehension was there, in my apartment, on stand-by, and so were the laundry and the dishes and the floors. At least in the hospital you don't have to clean up after yourself.

I staggered through a fog for weeks on end hoping I would miraculously wake up one morning energized, clear-visioned and my name being June Cleaver. As time went on I found it inconceivable how anyone could survive the constant demands, lack of sleep, not to mention all that CRYING! Breastfeeding Noël was so agonizing that when the Community Health Nurse came around, I begged her to set me up on an epidural that would, this time, numb me from the waist up! Suffice to say, "breast wasn't best" for Noel and I as it was choking, spitting, screaming (both of us), wrestling match that took place every two hours and lasted an hour and a half duration. I usually had to scrape this same meal off the wall in the adjoining room ten minutes later.

Enter... the Playtex Nurser.

I had done my prenatal reading and concluded that the emotional difficulties I was having were most likely what they called Postpartum Blues, but in my case they were more accurately… Postpartum Blacks. They hit so hard you could almost hear the wind being knocked out of me, but then you would have had to be listening very closely, over the sound of moving vans (yes, we moved twice before the baby was six months old) and the screams of my daughter from the pangs of colic.

Noël crocheted her little body into knots and shrieked for seven months straight for reasons I just could not figure out. The doctors patted me on the head and said she had colic and that my nervousness heightened her aggravation. Well, was it the chicken or the egg? All I knew was that after four or five hours of crying I would join in and we'd both be miserable for the rest of the day. I grudgingly tended to her needs suspecting there was no loving bond between us because I was so angry all the time. At times I was reluctant to even hold her because I wasn't sure I could resist the temptation to fling her over the balcony. I scrambled to find some kind of solution. I read all the books, tried all the sure-fire colic cures to no avail. Eventually the lack of sleep ground me down. One morning I jolted out of a deep sleep to realize that the baby had actually slept five hours straight! I thought, "Oh my god she's dead!" then turned over, twisted the blankets tighter around me and thought "yeah… but I got five whole hours of sleep"! Had my husband turned over and pried his eyes open for one second, he might have noticed a satisfied little smile on my sleeping face. Of course she was o.k. but the situation escalated.

My daughter was not at all a placid, happy baby. She had to be entertained and held constantly. Crying came easily to her and I spent most of my days wrestling with her difficult temperament. As for me, I was like a yo-yo that was permanently wound. I was worn out and keyed up at the same time. Anger surfaced alarmingly and as easy as and I struggled daily to keep from becoming unhinged.

My marriage already past the first stages of decay and I didn't anticipate any measure of recovery. I had no idea how Edward felt about the situation; sadly, I didn't even care. He was off doing his thing and I was home doing mine, or more precisely, my daughter's. I found the whole "new baby-new mother" synchronism too much to handle. Bottles, burping, bathing and barfing, what did I know about any of that? And I was furious that my husband was blind to it all. I don't get it, because I had a vagina, I had instant parental insight? I don't think so. My small household was filled with rage, indifference and despair.

This was the environment my mother arrived to when she came to see her granddaughter for the first time. A warm welcome indeed. Her visit was short and sweet (?) and she saw a whole lot more of me than I did of her. I was there more in body than in mind, and I guess it showed. She told me recently, that she knew there was something very wrong at the time, but she didn't want to interfere. A wise decision, I'm sure. I don't think I would have dealt well with any more conflict.

Noël got older though not easier to handle, but luckily, I became more seasoned to the situation. She was about 18 months when I began to feel a strange stirring, a mental invigoration. The fog I had been living in for so long was starting to dissipate. My crying spells lessened but were replaced by a chronically clenched jaw and a body that was braced for momentum.

A few years earlier, prior to Noël's birth, I met a couple from Los Angeles who were members of the Church of Religious Science. No, not Scientology, I had to assure my mother. They introduced me to their philosophies of which much was based on meta-physical and karma - type dogma. I already had similar beliefs and felt a real connection to these people. I studied a few of the affiliated texts available and found myself becoming immersed in the teachings of Ernst Holmes. I would talk about this divine wisdom I embraced, with anyone who listened. The more I learned, the more I talked. I began to feel a pressing responsibility to spread the good word. Physically, I felt like I was walking on water... not quite treading on the old terra firma. Mentally, I was impatient with anyone who didn't spiritually see things my way. I got to a point where I thought it might be my calling to move down to L.A. and become a minister for this particular doctrine. I decided that I was the master of my own destiny and could make anything I wanted happen. In fact, I had read some (inane) book claiming that with great concentration you could make clouds in the sky disappear. I guess you could call it a meta-physical exercise. I would lie down on the patio off the loft and stare at the sky, until I too, could achieve this great gift! Boy, were they gonna love me in L.A.!

And if that wasn't strange enough, I also took an interest in I Ching.

Very loosely put, this is like Chinese fortune telling done in earlier times with Yarrow Sticks (now with 3 pennies) and a bible-like manual. You toss the sticks, or pennies, and depending on the way they fall, look up the appropriate section in the text and find guidance in the passages contained. So the hundred-dollar question for me was: Religion or Radio? Which was going to be my life's path? I cannot believe I though this was the way to "my truth". As I was pondering my future, I began to feel great resentment towards my husband and daughter. I felt they were clipping my newfound wings. Finally, I had risen above the many months of apathy... I felt alive and with purpose. Powerful purpose! Now I had to figure out how my family fit into the picture? I was shocked when I realized that they were a factor in the issue. After not much thought I was fully prepared to leave them both if my destination pointed south. Then I began to grapple with the guilt of being such a lousy wife and mother. How could I have such disregard towards the people that cared for me, needed me? Well, I just did, and I could not for the life of me explain why. Just as inexplicable, I woke up one morning, began to tidy the house and came across the two books that had given me motivation for living for the past few months. I picked them up, glanced at the covers, and though "oh puhleeeeze! I'm gonna let some books tell me what to do with my life?"

With my new passions abruptly snuffed out, I was pulled back into the pitch of depression once again. My behavior was beginning to make me sick! I couldn't stand that I was so weak and that I never seemed to follow through with anything. How could I be so intense about something or someone, one moment, and so impartial the next? Why am I pleasantly content with my life at one point and then the next, am struggling with suffocation, fighting the urge to abandon my every circumstance? This cannot be normal! I cannot be normal!

I decided it might be time to investigate the benefits of professional help.

Insights into Manic Depressive Illness

• Rapid hormonal changes that occur during, and especially after childbirth, may trigger a depressive episode. Women with a history involving depression or manic depression are particularly vulnerable.

• Three to five days after a woman gives birth, her body undergoes incredible hormonal adjustments. Fifty to seventy percent of new mothers will experience a case of what can be called mild postpartum "blues".. They may exhibit signs of tearfulness, irritability, confusion, guilt and/or resentment. These symptoms will usually subside within a week. Ten to twenty percent suffer from a moderate depression that could last from 6 weeks to over a year in duration. The mother may show tendencies toward over-concern for the child's health and safety, to the point of obsessive or they may have difficulties in bonding with her child. Although many woman in these psychological circumstances feel inadequate and unable to fulfill their child's needs, they are unlikely to delegate tasks to others feeling that if they can't do the best for their baby, how can anyone else? This, then, can cause feelings of overwhelming responsibility and resentment. Fear can be a crippling emotion to these women… fear of the present responsibilities and, of course, fear for the child's future, which seems, to them, resting solely on their shoulders.

• A small number of women will experience what is called postpartum psychosis. This illness seems to manifest after delivery, often very rapidly. Like the mild and moderate type depressive episode, symptoms are usually exhaustion, agitation, irritability and extreme mood swings, but with postpartum psychosis these symptoms are abruptly accompanied by delusions and hallucinations. Delusions with a religious theme are common, as is paranoia. Even scarier than the fact that this illness gets worse over time, is the reality that seventy percent of women, who have gone through this horrifying experience, have no prior psychiatric history.

• Women with a predisposition towards depression or manic

depression will more than likely suffer from some degree of postpartum illness. That said, some women who do experience depression after delivery of a child, never have a recurrent episode.

Chapter Five: Therapy

For the most part, I have not stumbled through life unaware of the chaos churning around me. I suspected very early on that there was something wrong with me, or at least, my behavior. For the longest time, I wished there were "a pill" that would make my life "clearer". It was lost on me why I would loiter, with leaden feet, through periods of pallid haze, and then after a brief encounter with what I now refer to as "balance", be catapulted to the other end of the spectrum, where life practically blinded me with vivid primaries. Strange as it sounds, in those times, I could almost feel, hear and practically taste the colours in my surroundings. My appreciation of the esthetic was acute. Being yanked back and forth between these two polarities was to say the least, exhausting. And the aftermath of my daughter's birth had drained all energy and determination to go on as usual. I couldn't invision any kind of future for my family or myself with my fits of frustration and rage intimidating progress on anyone's behalf.

While looking through a community paper I saw a small advertisement for Parents in Crisis in the personals section of the classifieds. This was a support group for people who were having a difficult time with the day to day demands of parenting. Well... where do I sign up?

I felt dreadful enough about my conduct before I went to Parents in Crisis but after my first meeting I seethed in my wretchedness. I quietly listened to each of the women, in tempered voices, reveal what was happening in their homes and hearts. The circumstances were much the same in all households: not enough money, not enough time and too much to do. More than a few also had to struggle with the dead weight of a spouse who was incapacitated by injury or alcohol. These women were simply stretched beyond their limits. A handful had neither financial nor spousal problems; they were practicing dysfunctional parenting techniques inher-

47

ited from their parents. The children suffered regardless of the cause. These women screamed, hit and/or neglected the kids out of frustration. It was blatant to me why they were there, but where did I fit in?

My husband was healthy and had no substance abuse problems, and although I did all the day to day work of raising a small child, he truly loved his daughter and spent time with her when he found it. Our relationship was lacking in many ways but there was nothing volatile about it. It was more of a void than anything. Like two people in the wrong place at the wrong time that were responsible for the same child. At least that is the way I felt. As I've said before I really didn't know what was happening for him, we didn't talk much.

So there I was sitting in this room of marital and maternal misery feeling guilty because I didn't have a reason or excuse for my behavior. God, if anyone was entitled to be depressed it was certainly these women.

Driving home, I punished myself with my thoughts, "What is my problem? Why the hell can't I cope? I'm weak... and self-centered... and petty... and ungrateful... and... crazy?" I went to a couple more meetings but out of loneliness more than anything. With nothing much to contribute, except that I, too, was angry all the time, I started to feel like an imposter, so I stopped going.

Now I was a Parents in Crisis Dropout. Great!

The words "Mayday... Mayday" would pop into my mind every now and then, and at first, I was amused but being a devout believer of intuition, I eventually stopped snickering and realized this could be some kind of warning. So after much form filling and waiting (can you believe there was a three-month waiting list for "emergency cases"), I managed to get myself in to see a Social Services counselor in the area. It was the only route to go, as we couldn't afford the cost of a private therapist to help me figure things out. So once a week I went to a small impersonal office to talk to a stranger about very personal things.

I always felt worse after my session. I guess when you talk about emotions, they have a way of resurfacing, forcing you to push them down again. Kind of like heartburn. After the counselor asked me why I thought I needed to see someone, and I gave her the low-down on my recent emotional troubles, she began to ask me all the routine questions... How is my relationship with my mother... my father... my siblings?

Fine... Fine... Fine... I only got stuck when she asked me to tell her about my childhood. I told her that memories of that time in my life were vague and limited to a few.

I recalled that my mother would get stressed out now and then from having to look after four girls by herself. Being a pilot, my father was frequently flying in and out of various countries throughout the world. My mother tended to be impatient and demanding as a result of this sole responsibility. There wasn't time for "quality time" and I must admit, as a kid I was quite envious of the Waltons on occasion!

I'm not clear as to how it came about, but eventually it was this counselor's suggestion that seeing I had such trouble remembering my childhood, maybe it was because I was blocking events that were too traumatic to deal with on a conscious level. I'm ashamed to this day that her insinuation sent a twinge of hope through me. Frequently, she told me, people who have little memory of particular times in their life, have buried them beneath their conscious minds to keep from falling apart, to help them function. The problem is, she went on, is that these memories don't stay hidden away, they play out in unexplainable behavior patterns.

BINGO! That was it, I thought!

"From what you have told me about your mother, so far," she continued," I would have to say that she was emotionally and psychologically abusive. She was not there for you. You don't recall her ever having held your hand or telling you that you were loved, right? Well, she may as well have not fed you because those feelings of security and love are as important to a child's healthy upbringing as milk and vegetables. Now, as you are raising your own daughter, the feelings of loneliness and abandonment that you experienced as a child are coming back and you are retaliating with rage or withdrawing. This is why you have so many up and down moods".

Well as Pat Sajak says, "The Puzzle Has Been Solved!"

I was euphoric! At last I had an answer as to why I was so unpredictable, why I was struggling with motherhood and why at times I would shun any love or affection directed my way.

The next course of action was to do something that would give me strength, make me whole and put some balance in my life. At the counselor's recommendation, I wrote a letter to my mother telling her how I felt about this alleged abuse and how my life was fractured as a result. I thought I was putting the responsibility where it belonged... in my mother's unavailable lap. At last I could stop beating myself up, I wasn't alone in this mess. I posted the letter and waited for a response or, dare I hope an apology. I waited almost seven months. She never wrote, called or even had someone respond on her behalf. The counselor viewed this as an extension of the neglect and I tended to see it that way also. Why else had she not contacted me? She just didn't care and regarded the letter as little more than junk mail. I dug in my heels and refused to make the first move. Because I continued to have what I thought were merely emotional problems, I kept on going for therapy. Strangely, as the sessions went on, the counsellor's slant of conversation would lean more toward the subject of her upbringing. She then confided that she, too, had problems at home as she grew up. Her stepmother, apparently, beat her with a belt and locked her in a closet as punishment. With that intimate insight, the red flags began to furiously wave. When she asked me to consider putting my daughter in respite care (temporary foster care) until I started to feel better, I was completely shocked and distraught.

In a rare moment of clarity I realized something was not right. Until I figured it out, I decided that I would not go back for any more "therapy". I ended our session by telling her that I would never even think about taking such a drastic measure and got out of there fast.

I never went back, and she never followed up on the case.

In the following months, the estrangement between my mother and I began to diminish. We broke the silence and dealt with the issues. According to my mother, after receiving my scathing letter, she contacted relatives to get either confirmation or denial of the charges, so to speak. What she got were reactions of bewilderment. The responses were essentially "Where did she get these foolish ideas?" After intense retrospection, I began to reject this counselor's theory. It could have been a credible one, but, in this case, not very probable. But the damage was done. I found out later, that my mother was very distressed by my accusations and was overwhelmed with grief and anxiety that I would perceive our relationship in that way. She was so shocked, she couldn't respond. Although I now know that I was not entirely at fault for this fiasco, my guilt has not dwindled. That was nine years ago and I still feel the need to apologize. But at that point I was grasping at straws, something that made some kind of sense of the craziness of my life.

So now I was back to square one.

That summer, Edward planned a holiday where he would take our daughter, who was now eighteen months old, back to his hometown to visit his family for two weeks. I was working in a hotel lounge at the time and couldn't get the time off to join them. Then again, I thought it might be good for me to have a break. As the departure date approached, I became increasingly anxious and agitated. An insidious feeling, slowly creeping up on me displacing any good humour I felt about the bit of freedom I was about to enjoy.

As I drove away from the airport after dropping them off, I felt as if something in my head had short-circuited.

The next ten days were a blur of excessive drinking, with scarcity of sleep and food. I suddenly had the energy and inclination to paint all our pine furniture pink. At night my thoughts were concentrated on how I could beg off work early so I could sit down and party with the customers. It was in this frenzied state that I impulsively got involved in an extramarital affair. This was so unpremeditated and out of character for me at the time because for the previous two years I had no sexual desires whatsoever, and all of a sudden I've initiated an intimate relationship with a virtual stranger. Toward the end of the two weeks I began to dread the day my husband and daughter came home. I knew that I would have to face the music. I was sure that nothing would be the same again. My actions had changed everything. But, don't get me wrong - I wasn't repentant in the least. It just confirmed to me that my marriage was no longer viable and there was no turning back.

Things got very complicated as I tried to live two drastically different lives. My nocturnal activities consisted of sneaking, lying and cheating, washed down with an alcohol chaser. These are not deficiencies I normally display. I was out and out driven to do these things for, of all things, sex, at ill-advised times, in ill-advised places. If it wasn't so pathetic it would almost be funny, to feel asexual for so long and then to be acting out that way in my unsatiable quest for it. To top it off, I chose a partner who was totally unsuitable, not that ANY partner would have been. Regardless, I never before, nor have I since, been attracted to this type of man. What in the name of God was I doing? Dashing down the road to damnation... that's what I was doing.

And I picked up the pace.

At Ed's understandable request and to my agreement - and clandestine relief - I moved out. At which time I did one of the hardest things I had ever done... leave my child. At least I had enough wits about me to appreciate that she would be better off in her own home. She was only a year and a half and needed some semblance of stability, something that I would not be able to offer for a while. Not easily, I had to reckon with the fact that I just wasn't in the position, or condition, to adequately care for her. And as difficult as that choice was to make, I do not regret it, because I know it was the right, and only thing to do.

Insights on Manic Depressive Illness

•   At this stage, I can't say my point of view concerning therapy is particularly positive, or even educated. The thing I regret the most is that I did not seek help sooner. And though my first experience with a health "professional" was disturbing, it didn't stop me from continuing my pursuit for an answer.

•   If you are trying to decide whether you could benefit from some help, medical or psychological, consider these questions:

-      Has distress become your key emotion, and is it affecting your family, social and/or professional life?

-      Are you able to identify and handle your problems in an effective manner?

-      Do the stresses in your life have you often thinking about suicide as your only recourse?

•   My advice, if you have any of these concerns, would be to make an appointment with your General Practitioner as soon as possible. Your doctor needs to rule out any physical ailments that could be at the root of your problems. If you have no underlying illnesses or basis for your problems, be they mental or physical, then you have other avenues to investigate.

Other professional help to consider:

Clinical Social Worker: is a mental health professional, usually with a master's degree in social work who is trained to offer psychotherapy.

Family Therapist: a mental health practitioner who offers counselling services.

Psychiatrist: a doctor who specialized in diagnosing and treating psychiatric disorders. They are licensed to prescribe psychiatric medications.

Psychologist: a mental health professional who has a doctoral degree in psychology and is trained in psychotherapy, psychological testing and counseling.

- If you have decided to use a therapist or counsellor, make sure you find one who is familiar with the biological aspects of mood disorders even though you think it may not be applicable to you. You never know. And just to be sure you're looking in the right direction, go to your community mental health center, they should be able to recommend some good people in your area.

- When you have found someone to talk to about your problems, keep in mind, that when you are depressed and seeing a counselor (or whomever you've chosen), you may not be in a good position to be a judge of "good therapy". It might be a good idea to have a family member or friend go with you to your first appointment. Because this is an emotional situation it would be beneficial to have someone who can remind you what was said or recommended at the meeting.
  - At your initial appointment ask what kind of therapy they provide and how it will help your particular symptoms.
  - If they keep pushing you to "remember" events or insisting on a therapy, which doesn't make sense to you, get a second opinion.
  - Be concerned if you continually feel worse after your sessions than you did before.
  - Patients who get psychotic as part of manic depressive illness may do worse with "uncovering" kinds of psychotherapy.
  - Be suspicious if they keep telling you about their family problems and tries to connect them to your own.
  - Just because they have completed school, gotten a degree and have a license hanging on the wall, does not mean he or she is a good therapist.
  - If you do indeed find out that you have some form of mood disorder and have started a course of medical treatment, do not rule out

the benefits of therapy. Your behaviors may have made a mess our of your life - ruined relationships, lowered your self-esteem etc. - and you may need professional help in picking up the pieces.

• Above all remember:

A GOOD THERAPIST WILL EMPOWER YOU RIGHT AWAY!

Chapter Six: New Life

With not more than twenty dollars in my pocket, I wedged the three boxes of my belongings into to my old white Renault and kissed my tiny daughter goodbye. I wasn't going far logistically, just down the road really. But in my mind's eye I could already see myself having gone through the hardships that I knew were ahead, feeling positive and content in my soon-to-be, new life and eventually having Noël back with me. If those visions were merely illusions of exaggerated optimism, symptomatic of mania, then, in hindsight, I am grateful, because without them, I don't know how I would have pulled through.

Life was tight in many ways. I moved in with a co-worker from the hotel into a room the size of a large closet. On her twice a week overnight visits, Noël slept on a futon cushion jammed between the closet door and the end of my bed. I worked four nights a week at the lounge and continued my erratic behavior when I clocked out. I sure as hell wasn't winning any employee of the month awards and was ultimately laid off due to friction between my boss and myself. Now I was going to have to survive on a whopping $250.00 a month unemployment benefits, minus a hundred dollars for rent, that is. My diet consisted of starch, largely supplied by bagels and porridge, purchased because they were cheap and filling. If I was approached for a date, I tried to make sure there would be some kind of meal involved. It was really that desperate.

Eventually, the sullen force of depression showed up again, shoving me into my small room for protracted periods of time. My roommate was shocked to see this side of me; all she had seen so far was the "Party Girl". I didn't want to be around anyone. The person I had become involved with, made repeated attempts to see or speak to me. Once, he showed up at the door, and when I saw who it was, I practically recoiled in disgust. What had I ever seen in this person? Sure, he was a nice guy, but really, we had absolutely nothing in common. Where the hell was my head when I initiated this ludicrous combination? With considerable difficulty (on his part) I shut the door on that particular aberration of my life. And as they say: when the door shuts... a window opens. Actually it was another door... a door to a radio station to be precise.

I decided that I had better do something quick and drastic if I didn't want to end up on the streets living in one of my boxes. I pieced together a resume, thin on experience but full of potential, and dropped it off at a small radio station in the suburbs. I went back a week later and asked to talk to the Program Director. He was open to seeing me that day and when we met, he struck me as a funny, nice guy with a weakness for women. We chatted and he offered to introduce me to the News Director. We also hit it off, and before I knew it I was volunteering in the newsroom almost five days a week.

Having worked on a radio newsmagazine talk show years earlier, I had some idea of how to write and put together a newscast and of course my broadcast education was finally of use.

I will never forget this person's kindness towards me. He brought me in off the street and gave me a reason to keep going on. Not only that, he taught me everything I needed to know in order to swing a weekend news shift and he also became a much-needed confidante. When I wasn't doing work for him, I offered my time to anyone else in the station who could use it. Promotion, sales, reception, you name it, I did it. I ended up with a couple of part-time positions that gave me a full-time pay cheque, which was like a million bucks to me after existing on a hundred and fifty dollars a month for half a year. In time I moved out of my room and rented a not much bigger basement suite across the river, away from my recent, bad memories.

At that time, my estranged husband began to have his own personal problems. We decided that it was time for my daughter to come and live with me, especially now that I was beginning to establish myself. We had a legal separation drawn up, giving sole custody of Noël to me and sharing joint guardianship with her dad. I was thrilled the day I put her three boxes of stuff in my car, snapped her into her car seat and headed to our new home. It had been a long time coming.

Although we lived in a couple of really dingy places, every night after

I tucked Noël in her bed, I sat on my futon couch and counted my blessing along with my pennies.

It was a relatively peaceful time for me, especially since my moods seemed to have stabilized. It wasn't easy being a single mother, but I was so certain good things were on the horizon, I embraced the struggle, knowing every day I was getting closer to my rewards, whatever they may be.

My days were borderline hectic, they would begin at 5:45 in the morning when I would get ready to go on-air for my morning-drive traffic shift. The station had hooked up a broadcast line in my suite accommodating my need to be at home in the morning with my child. So in front of the microphone wired up through my desk, I would sip coffee, wrapped up in a warm housecoat, while I soothingly guided commuters in the rush hour traffic through rain, snow, sleet and hail. Noël would either sleep or watch TV quietly until I got off air. I would take her to daycare just before lunch, go back home, take a nap and then go into the station to do some voice work and afternoon-drive traffic. At 6 pm, I would leave the station, pick up Noël from daycare, go home, have dinner and get us both into bed at a decent hour. On the weekends while Noël was visiting her Dad, I did remote broadcasts to earn some extra money. I was living a common, wholesome, if not boring life. And I considered it an accomplishment.

Chapter Seven: Love and War

If one must go through life adhering to a personal motto, then mine would be: Always forward, never back. Without reservation, this theory has been to my detriment in certain situations, but I try not to dwell on the "would'a... could'a... should'a..." too much. I am more than satisfied with where I am today. But the path of my first marriage was greatly influenced by that, sometimes hasty, adage.

Dialogue between my daughter's dad and myself remained short in supply, and was usually limited to visitation with Noël. On the rare occasion we did discuss things of a more intimate nature, we fell into the roles of "confused victim" played by him and "stubborn evildoer" starring, yours' truly. I could see that what I was doing was hurting him and I couldn't explain my motivations or behavior to either of us. Still, I knew that I had gone through a lot already since our break up and it couldn't possibly be for nothing. Everything happens for a reason and I wasn't about to cash in my hard-won chips, return to the table and end up losing or just breaking even. I wanted to hold onto my gains and if separating our small family permanently was the next logical step forward, then I was ready to walk. Divorce due to irreconcilable differences, was how I thought of it. It was just a matter of time, really.

I don't think "happily-ever-after" was in the cards for us anyway.

Eventually Edward agreed that that was the reality of the situation.

Keeping with the storybook theme, a very important chapter in my life was unfolding at that time. Having a domestic pattern to my days again, I rarely went out socially, although it was required of me to make an appearance at a popular nightclub on occasion, to do a live broadcast for the radio station. It was on one of these nights that I ran into Stephen, a friend I hadn't seen in nearly six years. He wasn't quite my type back then, but I sensed, instantly, that time might have given us more in common. Over the next few weeks as we talked on the phone and over dinner, we realized something substantial was happening between us. While my relationship with Stephen grew, Noël's adjustment to the access schedule with her dad became difficult. I found she could not cope with the long periods of time she was away. I discussed the situation with Stephen and when the amount of child support I was receiving came up in the conversation he suggested that it might be a good idea to tackle both problems at the same time. I tried to work things out with Edward one on one, but I met with such resistance, I ended up seeking legal help. One afternoon, a few months later, while on-air, a man I'd never seen before walked into the station and served me with divorce papers. Surprised that I had been beaten to the punch, I knew it was inevitable and was almost thankful for the kick-off. But on closer inspection of the legal jargon, I realized Edward had obtaining sole custody of our daughter on his agenda. Although it was a bit premature, I had to know for certain where Stephen and I were headed in our relationship.

Much to my delight we were envisioning the same future and decided there was no reason to wait. The most important thing for me was to put more stability into my daughter's life and so we decided to move in together, as a family, as soon as possible. After strenuous negotiation, Edward's visitation was changed to every second weekend, while we waited for a decision to be made about the custody issue.

This arrangement was suitable to everyone, until a few months later, when religion became an issue. I had decided after incredible introspection that I would convert to Judaism, the religion of my husband-to-be.

This was not, by any means, a simple, uneducated decision. I had been to Israel years prior, had fallen in love with the country and culture, and this had sparked an interest in Jewish theology. At that time, I did not see a conversion in my future but knowing Stephen was not keen on marrying out of his faith, I now felt, with a wedding in the wings and prospective children on both our minds, it was something I needed to do. My future father-in-law joked, at my first meeting with him that it was a good thing that I was converting; otherwise he'd have to have me "rubbed out". I told him that was the most convincing argument for conversion I'd heard so far. I went through the Jewish bookstores and library voraciously scrutinizing anything concerning the tenets of the Jewish faith.

Because proselytizing is not regarded in Judaism, I had to meet with the rabbi three times to convince him that I was serious about my conversion. He finally agreed to be my counselor and both Stephen and I had to commit to weekly meetings in his office at the synagogue for eight months for guidance on how to incorporate Jewish Laws and traditions into our lives.

Now, not only was I seeking to retain sole custody of Noël, I also wanted the right to raise her, unimpeded, in a faith consistent with her mother and future siblings. I could write another book on the events that followed, but let me just say that the thought of Noël being raised as a Jew was quite offensive to her German-Catholic paternal family, and so, funded by the Duetchemark, the Holy Wars began.

It was largely a paper war, waged with legal documents and antagonizing affidavits as ammunition, along with a few court dates and incensed sessions in front of a family mediator. Never have I lived under such an oppressive volatile cloud. It permeated every aspect of my life and was very difficult to escape from, even temporarily. Even now, it is beyond me how I had the strength to see it through. There were moments of consummate despair; most of them verbalized over the phone to Stephen, in a long shrill string of expletives.

But with Stephen's support and guidance I managed to pull myself together and carry on. You would think that under this kind of pressure, I would have, understandably, suffered some kind of psychotic or at the very least, depressive episode.

But I didn't.

To make the proverbial long story, short, after eight months of Judaic studies and an appearance in front of the rabbi and elders of the synagogue, my daughter and I underwent the spiritual immersion that made us members of the Jewish faith.

Chapter Eight: Diagnosis

Life was looking pretty decent. I now had the conversion to Judaism behind me, a wedding date ahead of me and in between, I had managed to land a position as morning show traffic-reporter co-host on Vancouver's hottest new radio station. The station's format was fresh and happening which perfectly described the way I felt. I was doing freelance commercial voice-overs and my agent was getting plenty of auditions for cartoon voice-work. I had a lot of positive things on the go, so when those nagging negative feelings began to invade my thoughts again, I knew I had to cut them short. This time I knew I had too much to lose.

I was thrilled with my new job as it had been a long time dream to furthur my work in broadcasting and so I assumed that these unsettling feelings were derived from my upcoming marriage. I had similar experiences with my first marriage, which I wrote off as "cold feet" and realized later that I was subconsciously trying to tell myself not to go through with the wedding - it wouldn't work out. So this time around, there was no way I was going to say, "I do" when I wasn't sure "I would"! Once bitten - twice shy! Stephen agreed to attend pre-marital counseling before our big day. Through these sessions, I understood my issue was not that the marriage didn't have a chance, we were compatible, it was that I needed Stephen to understand that he wasn't marrying Mrs. Cleaver(stein). I intended to retain my individuality within our partnership and as far as children went, I liked them, at least the one's born to me.

Yes, I did want to have one with him, but I was no Tollhouse cookie-baking mother. In retrospect, I guess I understood that I had "problems" at times and they could be disruptive in a multitude of ways. I was starting to accept that there would be periods when life wouldn't be quite "normal" and I needed to disclose this deficiency and have Stephen's acknowledgement. The only time Stephen had gotten a taste of these "periods" was when I lost my job, along with twelve other staff, at the small radio station where I started in the suburbs. I went into shock for a few days but then came out of it, motivated by my decision to spend a year off trying to break into the freelancing market. Some months later, I sank under a cloud of brooding negativism that came to an acute head weeks later, sitting in the dark on the living room couch, well after two in the morning, crying hysterically because I thought Stephen was going to die before we got married and leave me without a child to remember him by. This was not a fleeting image... I seriously thought that was our destiny. I was completely distraught and it took days to rid myself of this notion. Stephen wasn't too alarmed by this episode. I'm sure most men would have been rather flattered. I was embarrassed by the whole scenario so it wasn't talked about much after. Other than that, things had been as normal as could be expected in our relationship; given the stress from the custody problems we were still experiencing. After a couple of counseling sessions, I felt Stephen understood where I was coming from, so we focused on the wedding which took place later that summer without a hitch. While our guests went back to their nice hotel rooms that night, the bride, groom and the four-year old went back to the condo to start packing for the flight to Cancun the next day, sans the four-year old, of course!

Unfortunately Cancun didn't live up to our conjugal expectations so we checked out of Mexico after five days and flew to Las Vegas, where we knew we would get the kind of treatment we wanted and where we wouldn't have to beg for service or spray for skittering cockroaches.

It turned out to be a nice break and when we got back to work I was so relaxed, I was practically giddy. But again the levity didn't last. It was so baffling! Here I had enjoyed this wonderful wedding, had come back to my wonderful job and everything should have been wonderful, right? Not with my "wonderful" history. For the next couple of months I continued on an apathetic descent, shifting quickly between bewilderment at my agitated, erratic behavior and then not giving a good Goddamn. I wasn't enjoying work as much and found that my capacity for concentration was weakening. I started to feel blunted, my sharp-wit slowly dulling. The thought of ad-libbing on air with my partner, which was one of my talents, paralyzed me. Life at home was no picnic. I was either horizontal or histrionic. Frequently I would fly into a rage over the simplest thing, such as having to find time to pick up Stephen's dry-cleaning. Just as often I would find it nearly impossible to get out of bed, I was inert with defeat. I was unrealistically demanding of my four-year-old and I am certain that is why she was always so grown up for her age. I became absolutely impossible to live with. I have wondered why Stephen didn't head for the "refund counter", seeing the turmoil started up again shortly after we tied the knot. Some say a marriage certificate will bring out a person's true colours. I suspect he was a bit concerned, but more so, perplexed.

Adamant to not undo the familial happiness I fought so hard to put together, I made an appointment with my general practitioner. I told her I thought I had premenstrual syndrome three and a half weeks of the month. I was irritable, picked fights and felt hopelessly negative about every aspect of my life. In addition, I was chronically tired, woke up every hour on the hour at night and when I got up in the morning I was racked with inexplicable pain. My doctor questioned me about recent events and my life in general. After she assimilated the information offered, she made her diagnosis: Depression. Depressed? Me? I was depressed? Having so much of what I wanted in life, how could I possibly be depressed, I asked? Great, I must really be crazy to be depressed for no apparent reason. She went on to explain what depression was, and that, in my case, it could be the result of the stress I had been under for the past couple of years or it could be organic, a chemical imbalance in the brain or even a combination of the two. Given my history, she suspected it was a combination of the two. To say I was shocked would be an understatement! But at the same time I felt almost triumphant! I knew it! There really *was* something wrong with me! There was an actual name for it, and what I had been experiencing for so long, were the symptoms of this illness. The doctor told me there were medications available to relieve these symptoms and hearing this, I felt my body slacken with relief. I never thought I would welcome this kind of news, but I practically embraced the doctor.

Thank-you, thank-you, thank-you!

But as hopeful as I felt, I couldn't deny my distress and apprehension at the situation. Stereotypical images of depression flew fast and furiously through my mind.

Would I get progressively worse? We've all seen those frightful images of lost souls whose dementia had sentenced them to live out their last years rummaging the streets for food and shelter. Were wayward shopping carts filled with another person's garbage in my future? What about my family? How will they react? Trying to digest the superficial information I was given about this mental illness, depression, I drove home, oblivious to the traffic impatiently working its was around me, sensing that I had only glimpsed the tip of the iceberg. There was so much more I needed to know and understand.

That would come later, after I had made the decision of whether to accept this diagnosis and fill my prescription. Ironically, I had always wished there were some kind of "pill" that would clarify my mind, take away the fogginess and irate commotion, and here, I had, a pound of "cure" right in my hand. But would I accept it?

Why are so many people opposed to taking medication, or more precisely, pills? We are not bothered by health advocates who tell us to buy and consume pills by the bottle-full in the name of physical well being. We gratefully wash down one or two Aspirin when we inflict upon ourselves a brain-bruising hangover. Would anyone deny an allergy sufferer an antihistamine? Where does this aversion come from? I realized that I couldn't afford the luxury of this particular hang-up because I didn't have much choice. I could not continue to live the way I had been so far, so what exactly did I have to lose?

Stephen's reaction was predictable. He expressed uneasiness with the diagnosis of depression, along with concern about taking pills on a long-term basis. Once again we sought the opinion of the therapist we saw before our wedding. We had come to respect and trust her and therefore decided we would act on her advice. I told her my biggest worry was of turning into someone I wasn't, I mean these medications do things to your mind, right? She rationalized that when I experienced the symptoms of depression, I wasn't really myself anyway! She also compared the scenario to one with a person using a crutch until their leg healed. Fill the prescription and give it a chance, the worst that could happen would be nothing-at-all, was her suggestion. So I did.

I don't remember the name of the first antidepressant I tried, but after a few days, I knew there was something wrong. The pills made me so high I tripped through the week, not remembering one day from the next. I skimmed over the highway to and from work, terrified I would be stopped by the police and have to explain why my car was hydroplaning on roads that were as dry as chalk. I called my doctor and she said, simply, that the medication wasn't the appropriate one for me and finding the right one would be a matter of trial and error.

Fortunately, the next one we tried, Desipramine, did work.

Although I started on a low dose and eventually worked my way up to a common maintenance level, I felt a difference within four days. The only way I can accurately describe these feelings is to say it was an inner stillness.

It was like when you were a kid in the playground, minding your own business, pushing yourself on the merry-go-round, and some big kid grabbed hold of one of the bars, and with legs like an ox, ran as fast as a horse while you were desperately trying to hold onto both your life and your lunch. Remember how you felt when that little demon, finally, got bored with the rainbow of colours passing over your face, let go and sauntered off to bully some other poor unsuspecting kid? Remember how you felt when the world righted itself and everything was in its proper place, your hair back on its scalp and the dizziness subsided?

That's how it felt. A blessed inner stillness.

One night, in the velour moments before sleep, I realized that I was healing. Healing from an illness that I didn't know I had. I was on the brink of balance and for this, I cried, not in the distressed sense, but appreciatively. I grieved for time lost and the reality of this penetrated my soul. Stephen held me that night somehow grasping the intricate depth of my emotions.

I was on the medication for about two weeks when I knew for certain, I had been hoisted up from my recent depression and as time went by, I was confident my turbulent emotions had been quelled long-term.

While things were back on track personally and professionally I discovered that the antidepressants did have drawbacks. I was tired a lot of the time and had to take a bulk laxative to help with irregularity, but my sleep was sound and I was actually rested when the morning arrived. The most serious side effect were the spells of dry-mouth. These were not easy to deal with especially in my line of work! But after a few months of gum chewing and water guzzling, thankfully this annoyance passed. And so did my job at the station. A couple of months later I was let go from the show for what I was told was a "lack of chemistry" between myself and the host. Strangely, in the weeks prior, I had been told we were doing an excellent job and to keep up the good work! Such is the business of radio and its mystifying ways. You never really know where you stand and are often at the mercy of egomaniacal whims. I packed up my personal effects and headed home to cry for a few days. I was upset, to be sure, but didn't sink into a devastating depression.

I could say I felt like a new person, three months into the course of medication, but it was more like feeling like my "real" self. Being unemployed again, I had the opportunity to mull over past events and during this reflection realized that most of the problems I had after Noël's birth were a result of my illness, exacerbated by postpartum depression. I concluded that having another baby didn't guarantee the same story line.

Maybe it was possible for me to have a healthy, loving relationship with a baby. For a long time I was haunted by the crushing weight of the anger and confusion I often felt when Noël was an infant. I swore that I would never inflict my shameful behavior on another child ever again. I felt so traumatized; I even made an appointment for tubal ligation at the age of twenty-six. I cancelled at the last minute.

Seeing I wasn't working and turning thirty-one that summer and had not wanting to have children after age thirty-two… it was now or never.

Stephen was starting to do well financially and my doctor confirmed that I was doing well physically, so I charted my cycles, hoping to time conception as close to two months after I stopped my medication as I could. I wanted another winter baby.

My doctor told me it was imperative that I get back on my medication as soon as possible after the birth, considering my predisposition to postpartum depression. Not being particularly fond of breast-feeding, I was more that happy to comply. My kid's chances of survival were much higher having a sane mother than the benefits of immune enhancing sustenance.

70

Insights on Manic Depressive Illness

•   If you, a family member or friend has just been diagnosed with depression or manic depression (also called bipolar affective disorder), the most important thing you can do is to look at the news in a positive way. That is, to realize that a problem had been identified and you can now take charge and turn your life around.

•   In its most simplistic definition, depression and manic depression are caused by a disturbance in brain chemistry. Because both chemical and emotional factors can produce these mood disorders, it is important to understand that stress or lifestyle can contribute to the onset and subsequent course of the illness.

•   Understand it is not all in your/their head, studies show that depression is the most incapacitating of all chronic conditions in terms of social functioning and is classified second only to "advanced heart disease" in exacting a physical toll measured by days in bed and body pain.

•   Have a friend or family member go to your doctor with you. They can understand and be far more supportive if they know exactly what you are dealing with. Ignorance of what's involved with this illness is counterproductive to all affected. Because you may feel overwhelmed with information and medical options, having some support at your appointment is beneficial even if only to retain information for future consideration.

•   Try not to be offended or influenced by negative, uneducated comments made by family or friends, such as:
"Maybe all you need is a change!"
"You just need to get out and exercise!"
"Change your diet, vitamins help me!"
"Don't fight it... just go with it!"
"Think positive!"

71

and worst of all: "Personally, I don't have time to be depressed!!"

• These comments are usually well meant, but they completely disregard the fact that depression and manic depression is a medical condition that requires specific treatment. And because these types of advisements don't work for the clinically depressed, they can end up making the afflicted feel like a failure thereby making the situation worse.

• Don't let the stigma of mental illness prevent you from seeking or maintaining treatment. There is no reason not to use available medical therapies if there is at least some chance they may help.

Chapter Nine: Siblings

I was the one the doctors should have smacked after the birth of my daughter. I was so traumatized by the experience that I wasn't even concerned whether the baby was healthy, let alone what gender it was. The only reassurance I wanted was that I was still alive and there was a shower within shuffling distance. Looking back, with guilt and regret, Noël and I unfortunately did not share many Hallmark moments. She was a rigid, demanding infant and I was the same except twenty-six years older. She wasn't a happy baby and I most certainly was not a happy mother. I had no means of transportation and even if I did, there was nowhere to go. I had no friends period, never mind one with a child. The fact that Edward and I were chronically strapped for cash didn't help matters either. The colic Noël suffered from was merely pressure on an already sore spot. But my biggest problem was the one I didn't even know I had. At that point, I still had no idea I had a depressive illness, let alone recognize the fact that I was in the middle of an acute post-partum depressive episode. No one around me did either. Two years later, during the custody battle for my daughter, in an affidavit volunteered by one of Ed's relatives, I was described as being strung out, unable to keep a tidy house and consumed with frustration. They were not far off the mark. What baffles me now was if they saw this aberrant behavior and were so concerned by it, why did they not help alleviate the situation? I guess they weren't quite sure what the problem was either.

I think people, who witness someone displaying depressive symptoms such as anger, despair, guilt, agitation, etc. and are not aware of the issue of depression, tend to view those types of conduct as character defects more that the symptomatic behaviors they truly are.

Eventually, when the legal squabbling stopped and the hostility between both parties waned, Noël settled in to a more regular family lifestyle. Having a mom and stepfather at home, seeing her biological father on her visitations and enjoying the playful stimulation of daycare, she became a more content and cheerful child. When the opposition and tension surrounding her religious upbringing petered out, she developed more of a sense of security. She was thrilled at the prospect of a brother or sister in her future. By drawing silly pictures of infantile faces on her version of my swollen tummy, she incorporated a baby into our family. Eventually she was jolted out of her happy daydreams by the realizing she would have to share her mom when the big day actually arrived.

After going off my antidepressants, I gave my ovulation cycle a few trial runs and later when a home pregnancy test proved positive, I was tickled pink. Throughout the first trimester I reeled with nausea and the enormity of what I had done. Both my heart and head told me everything would be O.K., but still there was kernel of doubt that would pop in now and then, sending me into a spasm of fear.

I would pour salt into the wound by obsessing over the horrible mother I felt I was when Noël was born. My moods began to swing, knocking me off balance time and time again. Of course "pregnancy hormones" had a lot to do with it, but it was more than that. I believe the hormones aggravated my depressive predisposition. Following a few raging, shrieking, head-banging-on-the-floor incidents, I asked my obstetrician for help. Fortunately I was well into my third trimester and until then had been able to cope with the upheavals, but things were escalating and it scared the hell out of me. My doctor reminded me that sometimes the benefits of antidepressant medication can outweigh the risks and that this was one of those times. It was clear that I couldn't continue the way I was.

I went back to Desipramine at the beginning of January '93, looking forward to my February 16th due date. Within the first week I started to regain both my equilibrium and confidence in my maternal responses. After all this was not my first time, I knew what to expect at the birth and from the early months of infancy.

My son Noah was born two weeks early after fourteen hours of labour. It was an average birth, except for the awe-inspiring epideral I requested at the incredibly painful end. When Noah was placed in my arms I was immediately overwhelmed with a crushing sense of love. And it was

74

easy; it just circulated throughout my body, surging my indulgent reactions to his childish demands.

I sat on my hospital bed, holding my terry-toweled cocoon for hours, drenched in peaceful baby boy bliss. When people came to visit us, I couldn't wait for them to leave so I could be alone with my son again. It was such an incredibly intimate experience. However when I saw what a big girl my daughter had suddenly become, I ached with both love and profound sadness. I would have done anything possible to turn back time, to give her the same tenderhearted welcome into the world her brother was receiving.

Four days later, at home in my own bed, I sat cradling a bag of frozen French fries and frozen peas around my hot swollen breasts. Was it possible that the pain of "drying up" was worse than childbirth itself? Right on schedule, I came down with a case of the baby "blues". As I sniffled my way through those couple of days, I was aware that the intensity of my emotions were superficial and that I wouldn't sink into the abyss. I was certain that I was going through a normal postpartum hormonal adjustment. Within a few days I was back to my old self.

I had different expectations of myself the second time around. Because of my tendency to become ill, either manic or depressed, when I am exhausted, Stephen and I worked out a nighttime schedule where he would get up with Noah every second feeding. We kept a supply of formula in a small cooler in the kid's bathroom where we could quickly warm a bottle under the hot water tap. It saved a lot of running up and down the stairs in the middle of the night. There were some pretty stressful days, especially since Noah, too, was blessed with the same god-awful seven-month colic that Noël had, but this time I dealt with it better. Stephen shared in the child-care too, for the most part, when he was home. I was always emphasizing the fact the Noah was "our" baby and was overzealous on the issue at times, but I would not play the martyr again, when I needed help - I asked for it.

After a couple of particularly difficult months with Noah, we hired a part-time nanny on the recommendation of our pediatrician. I was told that there was nothing wrong with our child, he was simply a high-needs kind of guy. Like his sister, he became bored very quickly, needed to be held incessantly, screamed during car rides and agonized through

75

teething. I couldn't believe God was putting the same woman through this torture - twice! But God is also a merciful entity, She invented the babysitter! I stayed strong and stable by having one come in three days a week, while I either caught up on some sleep, shopped or just stared at the walls. One woman we had for a few months vacuumed, dusted and sometimes even cooked, while Noah napped. I felt like I had my own "wife"! As Noah got older and easier, we had the babysitter come in two afternoons a week and later, only on Saturday afternoon and evenings. We also hired a housecleaner to scour the house, top to bottom, twice a month. This may seem like a lot of outside help to some, but I knew my limitations and I was not about to knock myself out and end up sick for months, or worse. Stephen was working around the clock and figured it made more sense, financially, to have him at work rather than scrubbing formula encrusted floors. Whatever our methods to stave off madness, they worked. Noah had as normal an infancy and toddler-hood as possible.

When he was about two and a half, we began to noticed that he wasn't speaking as much or as clearly as the other kids his age so we took him to a speech and hearing clinic to be assessed. His hearing was fine but his speech was definitely delayed, by ten months they estimated. Noah and I both found his inability to communicate extremely frustrating and by the end of the day each of us was worn down to our last nerve.

While his impediment crested, I declined into the major depression I described in the first chapter. As the illness progressed I became withdrawn from my family and couldn't meet their daily needs, especially my son's. With the help of the local speech and hearing clinic, we found placement for him in a children's speech therapy group, but it was clear he needed even more verbal stimulation. I find communication most difficult when I'm ill. I just don't want to talk to anyone, so it was almost excruciating for me to have to keep a slow, clear and concise stream of dialogue flowing between my son and I, as the clinic recommended. My patience was thinning and I realized I wasn't helping Noah's condition. How could I handle the responsibilities of being a wife, mother, and a speech therapist, if I couldn't even pull myself out of bed?

A new childcare center, built right around the corner from where we lived, put a sign up announcing its plans to open in two months. It was the perfect solution! At the time of the opening, I had Noah enrolled for two full days a week, with the local speech therapist attending the facility one of those afternoons to work with him and instruct the teachers on speech enhancement techniques. Four months of this program brought Noah from a ten-month to a five-month speech delay level. To this day he continues to learn new words, picks up much-needed social skills and burns himself out in the fresh air and sunshine. Could I ask for anything more?

Noah is gaining confidence in himself and embracing the world around him, while I am back on my feet with restored hope for the future.

Insights on Manic Depressive Illness

•   Children of parents with manic depression tend to blame themselves for the environment in their households. If things seem to be spinning out of control or stagnating in sadness, children will often think their behavior is the reason for the disturbance in the family's dynamic. And while the parent's treatment is the first priority, recognition of the children's suffering is crucial to their own survival, as it is common for them to turn to forms of substance abuse as a means of coping or escape. Ultimately, the family as a whole needs support and education, even after the mood-disordered parent has been diagnosed and successfully treated, in order to break dysfunctional patterns and adopt healthier coping strategies on a day to day basis.

•   You would think that the manic highs of a parent with a mood disorder would be easier to contend with than the depressive periods but, in fact, the opposite is true. Mania is not always displayed by a jovial increase of mood and activity; it quite often manifests itself in hostility and agitation towards those near and dear. Actions and utterances of the manic person can be profoundly destructive. Remember that, although you or the person you suspect to be bipolar, may not remember particular details of either manic or depressive episodes, such as comments made in a fit of rage or despair, or promises made with little likelihood of fruition, the people who live in the perimeter of these emotionally charged events usually maintain a painfully keen sense of recall. They need time and space to heal the wounds and justly deserve their own turn for tolerance and understanding.

•   I highly recommend routine be incorporated into the family lifestyle, for two reasons. For the parent who has the mood disorder, surprises are not high on their list. Of course, short of consulting an extremely accurate psychic over your morning coffee, there are going to be situations occurring that you hadn't envisioned, but if you stave off stressing out over the little things, then you may be better able to handle the whopper when it comes around. Plan your week in advance - know what chores or projects require top billing, what ones can be done when you get around to it and the ones that can be put off till a better time. Knowing what's expected of you reduces anxiety. Children benefit from routine also because they need to know their needs are going to be met on a daily basis and that when their parent does have a manic or depressive episode, eventually things will return to business as usual. Your illness, in a sense, will become a part of the routine and therefore less scary.

• Children of bipolar parents can be empowered by teaching them the ways to help out when the parent is ill. They should be told that their patience and obedience is extremely important in their parent's recovery process. They need to be taught to contribute by looking after household chores that need regular attention. Needless to say the chores should be age-appropriate. By helping out, I think they will not feel as "helpless".

Chapter Ten: Swinging

I cried, blamed, cried, complained, then cried some more, but those seven months of emotionally fused visits to Dr. Ryder, while I was off medication and pregnant with Noah, brought me closer to something I hadn't had before: a more accurate diagnosis of my depressive illness. Due to my recollection of everything in my past being a negative experience, my GP thought I had dysthymia - a chronic low-grade unipolar affective disorder. I couldn't remember ever being happy or satisfied. Although quite typical of people with depression (there can be a gray pall cast over memories), she assumed I had only endured depressive episodes. With Dr. Ryder, I disclosed details of my more shameful past. I confided my incidents of alcohol abuse, periods of rage and obsession, promiscuity and overall unpredictable behavior. These confessions revealed that I did not have dysthymia, but that I actually suffered from cyclothymic bipolar affective disorder, which are cycles of depressed, manic and normal moods. Considering the criteria required for this diagnosis, I realized I had been living with symptoms for at least half of my life. I cannot believe this illness escaped detection by the many professionals I had looked to for help over the years.

Occasionally I encounter a person who questions the validity of an impaired thought process as a medically identifiable disease. When I try to explain how I feel during either a manic or depressive episode, I think that while they may understand the symptoms, superficially, they don't comprehend the intensity, the way my life and those around me are influenced by these phases.

In my previous chapters, I did not delve too deeply into the characteristics of bipolar affective disorder's symptoms, I just wanted you to know how they affected the course of my life and how, maybe, you've had similar experiences in yours. This chapter addresses my symptoms, or mood swings in more detail, by describing my innermost feelings as I go through a depressive or manic episode.

Because depression is a psychiatric illness, when I am suffering from it, or mania, I describe it as being "ill"... just like any other disease.

My Depressive Episodes

One of the first things I notice, when this illness creeps up on me, is a sense of fatigue. It starts slowly as I drop a workout at the gym here and there, thinking I might be coming down with the flu. Then it develops into a bone-crushing exhaustion which causes me to become overwhelmed. As the fatigue sets in, impatience parallels. My relationship with my family becomes strained. I cannot tolerate having to do several things at once, as is commonly a parent's forte. I am not very good at being needed, even at the best of times, which puts me in a particularly difficult position as a spouse and mother. I begin to shut down emotionally and become unresponsive to the love and warmth shown by my husband and children. I am beyond reciprocation. Sleeping Beauty becomes my favorite sexual game, only I do not wake up at the kiss. All sexual desire had died. I avoid the act entirely or just endure it. Interest in hobbies is lost, along with my sense of humour. I no longer have the concentration level required to read a novel. Life becomes a bland visual of black and white. I become an expert in procrastination, including commitments made regarding my social life. The phone is infrequently answered by me and the doorbell goes ignored. I have even stooped to hiding in the bathroom hoping the potential visitor will assume there is no one home. When I do afternoon car-pool, I wait until I am certain the girls are ready and waiting so that I can zoom in and out without being noticed by any of the other mothers. Then, at home, I will complain that no one is friendly to me. I am so miserable, solitude is an absolute necessity. The fatigue can graduate to a level of incapacitation. I sleep all day and spend the evening riddled with anxiety about facing the one ahead. As expected, exhaustion and physical pain greet me in the morning. I cannot even make a fist let alone a sandwich for Noël's lunch kit. The decision between bread and bagel is insurmountable, so I don't even bother eating.

Juan Valdez is the only man I want to put my lips on. The most severe days are spent in bed, physically paralyzed, bound by this illness, waiting for decay. Sleep is my trusted ally, keeping my mind unpolluted by my wakeful profane thoughts. When aroused from my potent slumber, my mind is active, percolating with thoughts of how horrible a mother and spouse I am and how I have failed in my career and tainted everything I've ever touched. I expend great amounts of energy berating myself for these things, yet I can't find the strength to bathe anymore.

And I shower myself in guilt, about all the above, with my hot, incessant tears.

My Manic or Hypomanic Episodes

My manic episodes are revealed by two different attitudes, with agitation being the common denominator. One is an attitude of impatience and hostility. My level of tolerance, especially of noise becomes very low. A loud television volume, children's chattering and bickering, along with the clanging of cooking equipment are a sure-fire recipe for sensory overload. I sizzle and snap at every turn. A request for yet one more glass of juice can make me feel like exploding. I cannot handle the every day frenzy of things going on around me. Dinnertime is the absolute worst. I call it the "arsenic hour", and I wish I could imbibe in a drink of the lethal concoction, or at least slip a little into that juice request. All I want the kids to do is to sit quietly and watch TV. To hell with developmental play: toys = noise!

I am so very critical of my family, specifically, and life, in general. My words are as swift and pointed as darts, with hurt feelings being my aim. I don't want to be alone in my pain. Yet, I am not behaving in this way intentionally. I am aware of the damage being done, and as hard as I try, I am usually unsuccessful in extinguishing the inferno inside. There is nothing worthwhile in my life. I view my marriage as hopeless and my children as abnormal. No one can do anything right.

God help them.

My reactions to most situations are extreme, bigger than life. Physically, I seethe and bristle, fighting the desire to numb these feelings

83

with alcohol, the only substance I know will restore some kind of balance, by not making me as vulnerable to my environment. I used to wonder why I could tolerate Noël's colic spells after a night of too much wine at dinner. I guess when I was hung-over my nerves felt insulated.

The other manic attitude is a caricature, and exaggeration, of myself. I am not sure if my swollen ego is visible to others, but I feel a definite superiority. It's not mean spirited or demeaning, I think the sense of superiority is more directed at myself. I am looking, feeling and working better, and am wittier and smarter than I have ever been. I have so much to offer the world. I am agitated, this time, with optimism. My alcohol consumption is astonishing, considering my slight weight. I can consume incredible amounts without negative effects. I drink both in celebration of all my good fortune including what a wonderful human being I am and, once again, to settle my sense of being ignited. In social situations I tend to manipulate conversations, interrupting and talking a mile a minute. At least that's how it seems to me. "Why can't you just shut-up?" I ask myself time and time again, but I just can't restrain myself. I start many household projects and throw myself into new interests that ultimately fizzle out and become abandoned. The sunshine makes me flinch in discomfort and I realize I am getting headaches from chronically clenching my jaw. I am in a hurry to get from A to B, so I tend to drive faster. My dangerous behaviors extends to my sexual habits, where I can become impulsive, especially when alcohol is involved.

My depictions of the Jeckyl and Hyde- like expressions of this disease are not easy things to disclose. I have suffered much shame and guilt over these behaviors, believe me. I have always been strong willed, with both my feet firmly on the foundations of my beliefs. I believe I could be described as nice, caring, warm, honest and enthusiastic in character. To share experiences of these kinds of conduct with strangers and most importantly, friends and family, I feel at risk of permanent judgment. But the whole point of this book is to help people understand that these behaviors are symptoms of an ILLNESS.

That illness is bipolar affective disorder.

Insights into Depression and Manic Depressive Illness

Without getting too deep into the myriad of psychological disorders, there are essentially two forms of depression.

Unipolar Depression or Major Depression:

This is where a person periodically experiences episodes of depression that may last from 6 months to a year and can severely interrupt their life. They do not suffer the excessively elevated mood of "mania". Chronic mild depression is called dysthymia. Some dysthymics have lived years, if not their entire life, in a state of perpetual pessimism, boredom, fatigue and overall unhappiness.

The following symptoms are products of the biological disorder, Depressive Illness. These episodes are often triggered by situations such as the loss of a loved one, divorce, a new job, or a major move. It can be a gradual shift that you don't quite notice. You may feel you've become a pessimistic person or a loner. These depressive feelings can go on so long that the person begins to accept them as normal. When most people have good things happening in their lives, they feel content, positive.

When bad things happen to these same people, they feel disappointed and discouraged but once things look up again they bounce back to normal. For people suffering from a depressive illness, their moods may not necessarily be in sync with their environment. They are unresponsive to the positive elements in their lives. Even vacations or positive events do not alleviate their "down moods". Sometimes depressed people can be "cheered up" for a while but once this stimulation, such as attention or social situations, is gone, they fall back into that "mood". These people are suffering from what is called atypical depression. They don't seek, but can experience, pleasure for a time, while a person suffering from a moderate to major depressive episode cannot seek or experience pleasure.

Symptoms of Depression and Major Depression:
*   eating too much or too little, weight loss or gain
*   disturbances, sleeping too much or not enough

- chronic fatigue and lack of energy
- frequent crying, inability to concentrate, or make decisions
- feeling anxious or irritable
- feelings of guilt
- inexplicable physical pain or headaches
- cravings for certain foods or alcohol
- profound or prolonged loss of interest in life: eating, sex, hobbies, people, family
- no hopeful feelings of the future
- loss of ability to feel emotion
- sex becomes unstimulating or burdensome
- feeling closed off from others
- thoughts of suicide

Bipolar Affective Disorder or Manic Depression

This disorder is thought to be caused by a disturbance in brain chemicals that results in mood swings causing the sufferer to experience both depressive episodes and periods of mania. These abnormal moods are the opposite of each other in that when the person is depressed, they are in very low spirits, physically and mentally and that same person, in a manic phase of the illness, can be hyperactive, physically and/or mentally and even display a confidence and over-enthusiasm to the point of potential danger to themselves or others through their affected actions. It is important to note that both chemical and emotional factors can produce these mood disorders. Stress or lifestyle can contribute to the onset and subsequent course of this illness. The depressive episodes can last up to a year while the duration of a manic episode is from one to three months. Normal or near-normal functioning separates both. About ten percent of people with bipolar disorder suffer from a milder from of the illness called cyclothymia.

People with cyclothymia have up and down moods that each lasting for weeks to months. They do not usually develop into full blown manic depressive characteristics, although this has been known to happen.

The depressive episode of a cyclothymic can be mild, or moderate or major in severity. The manic episodes are called hypomania because they are not as intense or alarming as the full-blown form. Someone in a hypmanic state can usually function at work, home or in a social setting. The over-confident and euphoric mood of hypomania usually lasts a week. The sufferer will exhibit an increase in energy both physically and mentally. These mood swings are spontaneous and are not reactions to life events, necessarily. For the cyclothymic there are few truly symptom free periods.

One of the worst forms of cyclothymia is what is termed rapid cycling. The rapid-cycler has mood swings that are so dramatic in frequency that they sometimes go from high to low within weeks, days, or even hours. They feel like emotional puppets yanked every which way, totally beyond their control. Most episodes last approximately two weeks, but they can experience them up to twenty-four times a year.

Most people in a manic or hypomanic state do not recognize or acknowledge their illness because they feel "too good" for something to be wrong with them. It is usually a family member that sees clearly what is going on and initiates seeking treatment.

Symptoms of Mania:
*   decreased need for sleep
*   increased activity at home, work or school
*   increased sexual activity
*   increased alcohol consumption
*   feeling elated, euphoric or "high"
*   inappropriate laughter or humour
*   inflated self-esteem or feelings of superiority
*   overly optimistic
*   rapid speech that is difficult to interrupt
*   going from one topic to another with great speed
*   intense hostility and irritability
*   hypercritical and pessimistic
*   impulsive or compulsive behavior such as spending sprees, sexual promiscuity and rash decisions
*   delusional thoughts and hallucinations can be

experienced (commonly with a religious theme).

Symptoms of Depression:

- The symptoms of depression that a person with bipolar disorder experiences are the same as the ones felt in unipolar affective disorder, with varying degrees of severity.

Chapter Eleven: Into the Future

I believe in looking at the past, dissecting, digesting and ultimately learning from it. And that is where we should let it go. I can understand someone's need to know their "inner child" and how certain things that happened when they were young, might affect their lives today. I cannot, however, go along with the individual who uses these events or experiences as an excuse not to live the remainder of their lives to the fullest. If Freud had his way we could blame every unfortunate occurrence in our lives on our mothers, including plantar warts. But blame is toxic, it is a poison that seeps into your past, present and future, contaminating your chances at a pleasurable and prosperous life. You can only dwell on the terrible things that happened or were done to you for so long and then you have to let it go and get on with the business of living.

I am somewhat angered at the medical professionals I appealed to for their failure to recognize what I know now to be my obvious signs of depression. To say that I felt let down by the misguided counselor I saw during the time I had unknowingly suffered from postpartum depression, would be an immense understatement. Yes, these things have filled me with outrage. I can certainly blame them to a point for the years lost to this disease but they are not culpable for "ruining my life". They did not clearly see what the problem was and I went on to roller-coaster throughout the next ten or so years of my life. For lack of a more sophisticated expression:

Shit Happens.

I am overwhelmingly grateful that I do not have to forfeit anymore of my precious time here on Earth. Previous to my diagnosis I blamed myself for my self-destructive behavior. I thought I needed strife and trauma in my existence - why else would I create so much chaos just when I had attained a reasonable tranquility. It's a subconscious thing, I would tell myself, I am not comfortable with peace and civility. I must not be comfortable with, or deserving of, a normal relationship with a "nice" guy. That is why I am often angry or depressed in my personal affairs. I now know these assessments are not legitimate. Since being diagnosed, I can put together the pieces of my life and have them make sense. I can see why I did, what I did, when I did it.

These are definitive times for me.

Without the distraction of the intense highs and lows, thanks to medication, I am able to quietly discover who I am, now, and most likely was, all along. I have changed since starting my Paxil medication. Changes were once taken as a sign of approaching turmoil, but these changes are an unfolding of my true self. Some of the differences were to be expected. I am more productively creative now, especially since my concentration level has increased. I could not have written this book had it not. My thought process is clear and more concise, although I must admit I, at times, feel a mental slowness at times, but certainly nothing that causes impairment. I am a more social creature, warmly welcoming a dinner invitation and quick with a hospitable retaliation.

Strangely, even my appreciation of colour has changed. For years I have been drawn to the more somber essence of renaissance art. Lately the style and colours of Matisse and the like invigorate me. I have recently cut the shoulder length hair I feel I have been hiding behind for the past seven years, and enjoyed watching every inch slip to the floor.

My life, so far, has been so complicated; I am now craving simplicity in many areas. And with understanding and help from my family, I am on my way to finding it.

I don't have such high expectations of what I need to accomplish in a day. I no longer meet the prerequisites to be a Super Mom, and that's fine by me. I recognize that stress does me in, so I avoid it as much as possible. When asked if I have any allergies, I joke by saying I'm deathly allergic to "stress". "Aren't we all?" is often the retort. Taking an afternoon nap alleviates the tiredness I feel from the antidepressant. Someone with a heart problem needs to take it easy at times; so do I. And like the person with heart problems or perhaps diabetes, I too, have to take medication daily. Most likely for the rest of my life. Does it bother me?

Stephen once asked me about this, "How would you feel about taking these pills for the rest of your life?"

I asked him, "How would you feel if I didn't take them?"
End of discussion.

There is no choice for me, I will not go back to the way things were, or more correctly, weren't.

The transition from illness to wellness was and still is not an easy one for all influenced. When I married Stephen, I was attracted to the sense of strength and order he exuded. He is at best overly protective, and worst, controlling. He comes by these idiosyncrasies through the reflection of his parent's images. His father is the dominant figure in the family with his mother cast in the perfectly suited role of nurturer. It is common of Jewish culture for families to be so close knit they are practically the same sweater. They seem to need to know all details of the other member's respective lives. Many a phone call is placed between my husband, his siblings and my in-laws. A sense of security is achieved when they are assured, on a regular basis, that the others are safe and sound. We have the pleasure of merging with other close relatives to celebrate some of the Jewish holidays, where a lot of good food, laughter and personal updates are shared. I find these occasions amusing and gratifying at the same time. I want my children to be exposed to this milieu when possible; I want these to be a part of their memories. But frankly, this is not my frame of reference.

As I described earlier, my family does not share the same sense of intimacy. We are, when it comes right down to it, detached, but lovingly so, if that make any sense. At least that's the way it looks if you compare my family to Stephen's. As grandmothers, mothers, daughters and sisters, we are frequently on each other's minds and certainly indebted to each other by way of phone-bills. Greeting cards cross in the mail during holidays and birthdays and every now and then someone is blessed with a photo that was taken within the last decade.

Logistically we are as far apart as you can get in this country, some on the West Coast, some on the East Coast and many in between. It is rare that you will find all members of my immediate family in one household. In fact, the last time that happened was almost fifteen years ago. That was also the last time I had the pleasure of my aunt, grandmother and cousin's company. My first child has yet to meet any of them, let alone my second. When I lived in the same city as my biological father, during my high school years, we didn't exactly re-establish our relationship - not because we didn't want to - it just didn't happen, that's all. No offence meant, none taken.

Despite this we are still kith and kin. We just are not `in each other's faces.

I phoned my mother one night and asked to speak to Dad. She told me he wasn't home. "Oh," I said "Where is he?"

"I'm not sure, he was supposed to be home from a trip a couple of days ago... but he didn't show up." She admitted.

I was shocked, "You mean you don't know where he is and you're not worried?"

"Oh, he'll show up in the spring when the snow thaws!" she quipped.

This is my role model.

My mother wasn't exactly nurturing, but she did her job. She raised four decent, mindful girls who at the end of it all, love and respect their parents for their efforts. I have always admired my mother, for being such a unique individual even when I didn't quite like her. While my friends were hugged and kissed and cuddled, we were being superbly entertained with hysterical wisecracks, sprightly little jigs. I was always amazed at her knowledge of the lyrics to any song that came on the radio. And even in the heat of an aggravated exchange, I respected her razor-sharp use of sarcasm. She was very social and usually the life of any party be it bridge or dinner. I believe my father holds dear, these very things about her. She is not an easy woman to love. But I think he does his best by letting her know she is, through support and allowances. My Dad does his thing - she does hers. His occupation as a pilot gives her something she enjoys, solitude. She likes to be alone, not lonely... just alone, by herself. This is something I covet myself. I always have, for the most part. But there were portions of my life when the thought of being alone intimidated me. I always had to have a roommate, boyfriend or a date, someone around to help me define myself. Now, after all these years, in and out of illness, I am very comfortable with myself.

Of course I enjoy having my family around me, but what I crave now, after two marriages and ten years of childrearing, is a bit of space.

Room to move.

My children's demands are progressively diminishing, at least as far as

92

needing perpetual attention. And I celebrate this. It means that the time has come for me to be me again. Not just Mom or honey, but me... me... me. That sounds so mercenary!

But unlike most people, I have not had the luxury of living life knowing that I'm essentially going to be the same person I was the day before. I never knew what to expect from myself. At this point, I welcome each day with as much confidence as anyone. I expect to have fluctuations in my moods but the chances are good that they will not swell (or sink) to titanic proportions, like times before. I feel as though I am enjoying the calm after the storm. The skies are clear, the horizon is luminous and inviting and embrace everything life has to offer!

This is where another quandary begins. Yes, I have changed much to my husband's delight and in certain instances, I suspect, disappointment. During the time I was still undiagnosed, he was my primary source of support, making all the major decisions and often directing the resolutions of my conflicts personally or professionally. I am not suggesting that I was this child-like shell of a person who was a hundred percent malleable. I am saying there were many times I trusted Stephen's perceptions of situations more than my own. It was a co-dependant relationship in a way. I needed and relied on him like a crutch and I think he got satisfaction out of being the "protective provider of all things". Since my 'recovery', these roles have been vulnerable to the changes that are happening in our relationship. For one, I do not feel I can uphold the particular attributes of my former "part". I no longer have the motivation or the inclination. This doesn't mean I no longer need Stephen. I just need him in a different way. I need him to realize and accept that I can stand on my own two feet again.

I can and will make decisions for myself; take back control of my life. And ultimately that's what it all boils down to... control... and I have it... finally.

This manifests in our marriage by acknowledging that I need space. Space for me to be me. A large part of this need is satiated by Noah being in daycare three days a week. This gives me plenty of time to do errands needing unruffled expedience or to spend whole days slogging through the malls bargain-hunting. Discovering and fulfilling my dream of writing is by far my most important reward of this solitude. And although

Stephen would never begrudge me these growth experiences, it has caused him some measure of irritation and unrest. From my perspective, he feels he has lost sovereignty. For the past five years I have been a creature of habit, not far from home during the days and not far from the TV at night. Now when I decide to go downtown at night to meet a friend for coffee or a glass of wine, it flusters him not to know exactly where I am and when I'll be home. He is a creature of precision, who lives by fifteen-minute segments carefully arranged in his daytimer. I can scarcely find my daytimer. Saturdays are his day with the kids. It is the only day of the week I savor an extra hour or two of sleep. When I do get up, I have the whole day to do whatever I want. I am not required to pour even one glass of juice. On those days I go shopping or roller-blading, stop for coffee or sit in Chapter's bookstore for three hours going through the latest magazines. Sometimes I spend some extra time with my daughter. My point is, that I find not being on someone else's agenda completely liberating, to the degree of exhilaration. Stephen's inspiration for getting through Saturday… is Sunday. That's his "free day".

Because he doesn't comprehend why I need time alone, I stress that it helps me define myself as an individual. But he's of the thought that once you're married, your partnership should be your primary concern, that you grow together, experience life as a couple.

I beg to differ.

As the old joke goes: two lovers come together, get married to become one… but which one? I believe each person is an individual first and then they share "coupledom". I think there is hope for us, because despite our interpretations of how one should live life within a marriage, we are kept together by a nucleus of love for each other and our children. And through straightforward communication, I also believe we can achieve a common ground. Communication is fundamental to the happiness of the family dynamic, and especially so in one that has a member suffering from a mood disorder.

During my last major depression, described in Chapter One, I was compelled to explain my illness to my daughter. Not sure how one talks to a child about these delicate subjects, but knowing my daughter to be mature and comprehensive of other grown-up matters, I decided to take the direct approach. I did not want to take the chance that she might think she was

94

responsible in any way. She already blamed my bouts of unhappiness on herself as it was.

I explained that I had a disease called `manic depression'. I thought it would be easier to understand that than the term `bipolar affective disorder', and that I suffered from an episode of this disease for the last month or so.

"A DISEASE??" she cried.

"Yes," I said, "A disease of the brain."

"A disease of the BRAIN?? Oh Mommy are you going to die?"

"No," I replied. "I just look like I will!"

I tried to keep the conversation as light as I could. I went on to tell her the way I've been behaving lately was because my medication wasn't working the way it was supposed to and that I had to go off it for a while before I tried a different one. I talked about the way people act when they're depressed and that I was crying, angry and stayed in bed all day because I was sick with this illness called depression. She indicated that she understood so far. I saw her shoulders come down a notch or two when I assured her that it wasn't anything that herself or her brother had caused. Although, when I was sick like this, they needed to remember that noise and obstinance was not the way to go for a while. Then I told her that the good thing about this illness is that there is medication I can take that will make me better again.

"You have to take MEDICINE for your BRAIN?"

"Yes," I said. "Noël, you know the pills I have been taking everyday for the past three years... my 'Crazy-Mother Pills'. "Yes," she answered.

"That's them," I said. "...I just need new ones!"

"OHHHH!" Down went her shoulders again, "So... what's on TV tonight?"

Life goes on.

Insights to Manic Depressive Illness

Getting Better... Staying Better:

• Is life supposed to be fair? Is it supposed to be easy? We know the answer to those laments. But for the person with a mood disorder, this mortal coil has more twists and turns to get through than the average human is required to negotiate in a lifetime. A simple, mundane activity can throw a person with manic depression for a complete loop whether they are in a depressed or manic phase. And the brief taste of normalcy between these polarities can be as painful as they are sweet. They never seem to last long enough. Life with manic depressive illness is confounding, to be sure, but consider what it is like to have the symptoms I have described throughout the book, touching your life without even knowing the root of the problem. Frankly, I have found it immeasurably easier to live with the "devil I know... than the devil I don't know"! Prior to my diagnosis, I lived an emotional enigma. I had no idea what to expect from one day to the next, was afraid to plan ahead for fear of looking like a flake. At times I thought I needed to have a "life plan" and stick to it no matter what! Personal goal definition - which is what anyone, who is successful, has. Except me. For God's sake, I couldn't commit to a breakfast cereal, and I was utterly mortified by this "fickleness".

Now I strive to take things one day at a time. I'd heard that saying for so many years and it escaped me how people could be so cavalier, so bloody laid back about their lives, their futures! Then I realized it was a choice. You decided that you were not going to sweat the small stuff and to be flexible about the situations that life presented. You chose to worry only about today, not next week or next month. But what I didn't realize at the time, is that it wasn't simply a choice for me; when I was ill, I couldn't control the chemical upheaval in my brain. After recognizing and understanding the effect bipolar illness had on my life I knew I did have a choice, and I made it. I was going to educate myself as much as I could about this illness, get better and 'get a life'.

Getting Better

•   The first step to "getting your life back" is to find out what is wrong. Knowing a general practitioner or family doctor allots approximately fifteen to twenty minutes per patient, it's not surprising that they are looking for the physiological, not psychological. When asked what the problem is, patients struggle to explain symptoms that end up sounding like physical ailments such as "I have pain in my stomach, head, back, heart". Those are the complaints the physician hears, but what he doesn't hear are the emotional symptoms. So when you see your doctor, of course explain how your body is feeling, but be upfront about what's going on in your head too.

•   One thing to keep in mind is that untreated depression can eventually cause physical illness and physical illness, such as arthritis, can also cause depression. I find that it is a good idea to write down the things you want to share with your doctor because sometimes you can forget vital information when you are going through your "interrogation".

•   If your doctor suspects that you are suffering from a mood disorder, he will make the diagnosis by checking your symptoms and comparing then to a standard set of criteria in the DSM IV R. This is the Diagnostic and Statistical Manual of Mental Disorders, which lists the symptoms, intensity and duration of particular mental illnesses'. Your family doctor can assess whether you could benefit from antidepressants or other medication for mood disorders and prescribe what he/she thinks is appropriate for your condition. You may decide to seek the opinion and advise of a doctor who specializes in mental health problems such as a psychiatrist, who is also certified to prescribe medication. Not only can a psychiatrist work with a patient to help them understand their illness, they can counsel him/her on how to live with the illness and avoid situations that may lead to further episodes. Efforts can be complicated in making a diagnosis because depression and manic depression is not always a singular problem. Many people have compounding issues that can mask the underlying problem of depression such as:

- Drug or alcohol addictions
- Eating disorders
- Panic or anxiety attacks
- Obsessive/compulsive disorders

If you feel you have a drug or alcohol addiction, you may need to detoxify before you begin treatment.

• As you can see, in order for your doctor to get a clear picture of what is going on, it is very important to discuss all things that are troubling you, body and mind. If your doctor does indeed think you are tormented by a mood disorder, he/she will explain that people with mood disorders have a biochemical imbalance, in one or more neurotransmitters (which are chemical messengers in the brain) that send information from one nerve ending to the receiving end of another. These chemical messengers control your appetite, sleep habits and of course your moods, among other things. Family history, biochemical and psychological makeup and any recent changes or stress' (childbirth, death of loved one or loss of job) in the patient's life are taken into consideration when making a diagnosis. For some, episodes of mental illness happen for no conspicuous reason.

• Statistics say, at least one in five people will experience a depressive episode in their lifetime. and that more than one percent of the population suffers from manic depressive illness because of the lack of public awareness and stigma attached to mental illnesses', many people afflicted with this disease have no idea their lives are being torn apart by the devastating symptoms. Some ignore the signs out of shame and embarrassment. The real crime is that, although these mental illnesses cannot be cured, eighty percent of patients taking proper medication will experience a reduction in episodes, duration or intensity of their symptoms.

• The biggest obstacle in the way of recovery for people with mood disorders is misdiagnosis. Most people make at least four or five visits to various doctors before they get a proper diagnosis and effective treatment. It is unbelievable that these same people have probably lost ten to fifteen years of quality life due to this illness and its ambiguous nature.

•   If your doctor concludes that you have been experiencing symptoms of depression or manic depression, his next job is to find an effective course of treatment. In the past, twice as many tranquilizers and sleeping pills were prescribed as proper medication to treat mood disorders. Even when the right medication was prescribed, it was often given in too low a dosage to fully correct the condition.

•   Often, a skilled doctor will recognize that a patient is suffering from a mood disorder and will proceed to educate them in the basics of these illnesses. The doctor goes on to prescribe what he hopes to be an effective treatment, but the patient himself stands in the way of recuperation. Fear of the stigma attached to this particular illness can be the cause. People tend to see their depressive or manic depressive episodes as weakness of character.   Society commits a profound injustice by telling sufferers to "cheer up", "snap out of it" or "stop being so lazy" and other misguided advisements. It is akin to telling those who suffer from heart problems or cancerous conditions to "just get it together and you'll be fine!"

•   Some people can't swallow the reminder that they are suffering from a mental illness every time they have to take their medication. They would rather live in the ruins of denial.

•   Cost can be another factor in not receiving proper treatment. Many people cannot afford the costly medications and/or the therapy to help put their lives back on track.

•   One of the most common reasons people with this type of illness will not commence with treatment, or discontinue prematurely, is because of the side effects caused by the medication. These effects can be a deterrent to someone who does not realize that they usually dissipate after time, or that the alternative, life with this disease left untreated, is much worse. Many will give up on their quest for wellness after only a few weeks on medication because they can't see over the wall of time it takes to feel improvement, which is within four to six weeks for noticeable relief and possibly four to six months for full recovery. It is quite common for a patient to try a few different medications on a trial and error basis, depending on individual symptoms, brain chemistry and tolerance to the side effects.

- The following are medications used in the treatment of mood disorders:
- Lithium
- Antidepressants
- Major/minor tranquilizers
- Electroconvulsive Therapy

- The common goal of the following treatments is to restore the chemical balance in the brain.

Lithium:

Lithium Carbonate is a naturally occurring salt that is found in minute amounts in the human body. Although lithium is used to treat both manic and depressive episodes of bipolar affective disorder, it is usually used to stabilize moods, hopefully making them less frequent and severe and shorter in duration.

It can take several weeks, several months to start working. Some side effects (blurred vision, increased thirst, weight gain, muscle weakness or hand tremors, etc.) can occur early in treatment but most disappear with time.

Because a maintenance level of lithium can be a difficult dose to achieve and sustain, regular blood tests are required to determine levels. If the dose of lithium is too low... it won't work. Levels that are too high are dangerous.

Contact your doctor immediately if you suddenly experience any of the following symptoms: slurred speech, flu-like symptoms (vomiting, nausea or diarrhea), weakness, drowsiness or severe trembling.

*Certain dietary precautions are required when taking lithium.

Antidepressants:
Among other theories, depression is thought to be caused by a deficiency of certain neurotransmitters (chemicals) in the brain. The most common chemicals involved are: serotonin, epinephrine and norepinephrine. Antidepressants boost the level of these chemicals that travel from one nerve ending to the other by hindering the enzymes that act as a clearing house between receptors. This process is called "uptake inhibition".

Tricyclic antidepressants: first used in the 1950's, such as amitriptyline (Elavil), desipramine (Norpramine) and imipramine (Trofranil), are used to raise levels of norepinephrine and serotonin. These medications can cause side effects like dry-mouth, constipation, sedation, dizziness, weight gain and urinary difficulties.
Selective Serotonin Reuptake Inhibitors (SSRI's): are the newest category of antidepressants. Common brands include: fluoxetine (Prozac), paroxetine (Paxil) and sertraline (Zoloft). The main function of this medication is to keep serotonin levels from being re-absorbed. Side effects may include dry mouth, dizziness and sexual dysfunction. These effects usually go away after a few weeks and are not as troublesome as with tricyclic medication.

Monoamine Oxidase Inhibitors (MAOI's): stop an enzyme called 'oxidase' from breaking down neurotransmitters like serotonin and norepinephrine. Common names are phenelzine (Nardil) and tranylcypromine (Parnate). *Patients who take MAOI's require strict dietary control.*

Your doctor may also consider prescribing one of the following newer medications:
bupropion (Wellbutrin) -affects dopamine levels.
trazodone (Desyrel) - affects serotonin receptors.
venlafaxine (Effexor) - affects serotonin and norepinephrine levels.
nefazodone (Serzone) - affects a certain serotonin receptor.
Because each type of antidepressant has a different effect on neurotransmitters, you will be prescribed a medication, taking into account your specific symptoms and medical history.

101

**It is very important to never mix medications without the consent of your doctor.

Major/Minor Tranquilizers

Major tranquilizers (neuroleptics such as clonazipame - Clonopin): are used in treating the patient with mania, anxiety and/or hallucinations and delusions. These medications may take up to eight weeks to work so severe cases are sometimes treated by injection which takes effect within a few hours or days.

Minor tranquilizers such as loazepam (Ativan) or diazepam (Valium)) are taken to relieve anxiety symptoms and are effective immediately. It should be noted that these medications can be addictive if taken on a daily basis for a prolonged period of time.

*Do not mix with alcohol, the interaction could be fatal.

• Sixty to eighty percent of patients who take antidepressants as directed by their doctor will get relief from their particular depressive or manic symptoms, within four to six weeks. Sometimes a medication prescribed does not work or the patient finds that the side effects are intolerable, then the doctor or psychiatrist will either change the dosage of the same medication, try a different drug from the same group or prescribe an antidepressant from another group. It is not at all unusual for a doctor to try a combination of medications from both groups.

• Mental illness is as unique to each patient as his or her fingerprints - no two people have the same brain chemistry - what works for one patient will not necessarily work for another. In the case that your doctor has to try a number of different antidepressants, depending on the medication, you may have to go through a `wash-out' period before you begin a new drug.

Electroconvulsive Therapy

Electroconvulsive therapy is also known by many as 'electric shock therapy'. The actual procedure is not as gruesome as it once was or was thought to be. The procedure is thought to change the function of chemicals in the brain. In cases where a patient is experiencing severe depression or mania and cannot wait the four to six weeks for medications to start working, electroconvulsive therapy can be used when immediate intervention is needed. Patients can start to feel better after two or three treatments, with full recovery time being after approximately eight to twelve treatments. This form of treatment is also used when someone with a severe mood disorder does not respond to medical and/or psychotherapy, or who cannot tolerate the side effects of psychotropic drugs. One of the side effects of ECT is short-term memory loss.

Staying Better

If you have been troubled with symptoms of a mood disorder, finally getting an accurate diagnosis may seem like the end of an extended nightmare. But once your doctor has found a treatment whether some form of psychotherapy and/or medication, that works for you, you are faced with the reality of proactively living with this illness.

• It's important to remember these medications do not cure the illness. They only help control the frequency and severity of it.

• Some people suffer from recurrent episodes of depression and/or mania and others may have only a couple during their lifetime. How long you stay on medication may depend on what category you fall into. If you have had only one episode or they come infrequently, you may decide to take medication only when you are symptomatic. Those who have a history of severe mood swings may want to consider long-term treatment.

• A maintenance level of medication may need to be adjusted from time to time because of illness or extreme stress in the patient's life.

• Recognize symptoms of an impending manic or depressive episode. Be honest with yourself and family, let them know how you are feeling and what they can do to help.

• Important decisions, commitments or obligations should not be made when you are experiencing either phase of manic depressive illness.

• If you are experiencing a depressive episode, try to lower expectations of yourself. Do only what requires immediate attention and slowly get through the rest. Accept help from others when offered. Use your `up' time to take care of things that were neglected during your `down' time at home and at work - but don't get carried away.

• If you feel you are becoming manic make sure to take some 'quiet time' and stay away from caffeine or other stimulants.

• Do not drink alcohol when depressed, manic or on medications. Drinking when depressed can make things worse and when you are manic there is a tendency to over indulge. Of course alcohol depresses the Central Nervous System which then counteracts the effect of antidepressant medication.

• Always contact your doctor if you feel that your treatment or medications are not working.

Glossary:

Agitated Depression (a.k.a. "mixed state"): depressive symptoms - apathy, hopelessness, anger etc. - that is accompanied by agitation, anxiety and restlessness.

Anticolinergic Effects: this is the name for the side effects that occur due to the blockage of the neurotransmitter acetycholine caused by a medication. The most common ones are constipation, dry mouth and blurred vision.

Affective Disorder: a disorder in which one's mood is prone to change to extreme sadness or elation or swing between both. This term is used in reference to both depression and mania.

Anhedonia: the inability to experience pleasure, usually the prominent symptom of depression.

Anorexia Nervosa: an eating disorder in which the sufferer has an extreme fear of becoming fat to the point where they refuse to eat adequately even after their weight drops below guidelines.

Bipolar Disorder: episodes of major depression alternating with mania.

Bulimia: an eating disorder that involves binging and purging through self-induced vomiting or laxative abuse.

Clinical Depression: a depression where symptoms are severe and chronic enough to require medical intervention.

Cyclothymia: a form of manic depression that has lasted at least two years in which moods cycle between depression (inactivity and fatigue) and mania (over-activity and hyper-confidence).

Depression: a mood disorder where the sufferer has persistent feelings of sadness, despair and/or hopelessness. Lethargy, inexplicable pains and an inability to experience pleasure usually accompany these moods.

Drug Interaction: an interaction between two drugs when taken at the same time. This can result in the decreasing or increasing of the effects of one or both of the medications.

Hypomania: a form of manic depression where moods swing between severe depression and mild mood elevations with increased activity.

Lithium: a natural salt that is used in the medical treatment of manic depressive disorder.

Maintenance Treatment: the continuation of medical treatment to help prevent or reduce occurrence and severity of further mood swings.

Mood Disorder: a disorder that is characterized by shifts in one's mood - from extreme sadness to euphoria or irritability.

Neurotransmitters: the chemical substance that transmits nerve impulses, or messages, between synapses, which are the microscopic gaps between nerve endings.

Obsessive Compulsive Disorder: a disorder demonstrated by the inability of the sufferer to resist certain repetitive thoughts or behaviors such as constant counting, hand-washing, checking or even stealing.

Panic Disorder: a form of anxiety disorder characterized by intense fear felt mentally and physically for no obvious cause.

Postpartum Depression: a severe and long lasting depression that affects some women after childbirth.

Psychomotor Agitation: excessive, rapid physical (motor) activity that is the effect of extreme mental activity.

Psychomotor Retardation: exceedingly slow physical (motor) activity that is the result of mental inactivity.

Psychopharmacology: the study of the effect of drugs and medicines on psychological processes.

Psychotic Depression: a depressive episode with psychotic features such as delusions and hallucinations.

Selective Serotonin Re-uptake Inhibitor (SSRI): an antidepressant medication that impedes the re-uptake of serotonin into the nerve receptors.

Serotonin: a neurotransmitter found in the brain that is believed to cause depression when at low levels.

Tricyclic Antidepressant: a type of antidepressant made of a three ring chemical structure that is usually prescribed for major depressive disorder. This is considered to be one of the "older" antidepressants.

Unipolar Depression: major depression that, unlike bipolar depression, does not alternate with mania.

Wash-Out Period: the time between the discontinuation of one drug and the initiation of another. During this time the body rids itself of any traces of medication. The period of time recommended depends on the drugs involved but is usually between one to two weeks.

Karen Kennedy

About the Author:

Karen Kennedy is a radio/television broadcaster who has worked and lived in Vancouver, B.C. for 15 years and has recently moved to Sarnia, Ontario where she is a morning-show host on CFGX 99.9 The FOX FM.

Born in St. John's, Newfoundland, she's lived in many areas of Canada and has worked in various industries from broadcasting to hotel/restaurant to painting nuts, bolts and stretches of pipe at oil refineries in Alberta. Her adventurous and restless nature compelled her to travel though parts of the U.S., Europe, the Middle East and the Bahamas.

While "Confessions of a Swinger" is her first plunge into the literary lake, she hopes to continue writing and is currently working on her next endeavor which addresses, among other issues, the Canadian judicial system and its impact on divorcing families in turmoil.

ISBN 141200284-2